Home Preserves

Home Preserves

Jackie Burrow

Sundial

Contents

First published in 1979 by Sundial Books Limited
59 Grosvenor Street, London W1

Third impression, 1980

© 1979 Hennerwood Publications Limited

ISBN 0 904230 81 3

Printed in England by Severn Valley Press Limited

INTRODUCTION

A larder stocked with rows of jars containing home preserves is a very rewarding sight, which reflects a renewed interest in healthy, natural foods and old cooking skills.

The main purpose of preserving is to keep certain foods for later in the year when they are out of season. Originally this was a necessity, to provide food for the lean winter months.

Nowadays there are many reasons why we preserve foods. It is economical to make use of cheap, seasonal foods, especially when there may be gluts of certain fruits and vegetables. Many people now grow their own produce, and with more and more 'pick your own' farms there is no reason why cheap ingredients should not be found.

Home preserves are therefore usually cheaper than manufactured varieties and undoubtedly superior in quality – the natural flavours, aromas, colours and textures are evident as soon as the jars are unsealed. You can also make recipes to your family's likes and dislikes, and try out unusual flavour combinations that are unlikely to be found in a commercial product.

Making your own preserves is also very satisfying and fun to do. As they often take some time to make, the whole family can be happily involved – they will certainly not be able to miss the delicious aromas that pervade

the house during preserving time. The store cupboard brimming with jars is a constant source of pride and pleasure – to look at, to enrich the flavour of numerous meals and they make wonderful presents.

The recipes in this book preserve fruits and vegetables to give delicious jams, jellies, marmalades, conserves, bottled fruits, drinks, pickles, chutneys and sauces. Many are traditional favourites, but there are also some new ideas to try out.

STORING PRESERVES
Although most preserves keep well for over a year if properly sealed and stored, do not keep them for too long. The flavour will always be better if used within the year and then the space will be available to preserve the next season's produce.

JAMS

Home-made jam is one of the tastiest ways of preserving fruit, and although jam-making is not difficult, it does call for a good understanding of the basic principles involved to obtain perfect results.

Jam is a preserve of cooked fruit boiled with sugar until set. A jam must contain enough acid and pectin (a natural gum-like substance present in fruit in varying proportions) in order to set properly and sufficient sugar to keep properly.

Pectin forms a gel when boiled with sugar and acid, and on cooling sets to give jam its characteristic soft, spreading consistency. Some fruits are naturally richer in pectin and acid than others, therefore recipes will vary accordingly to obtain a good setting jam.

Fruits with a high pectin content are cooking apples, black and red currants, gooseberries, damsons, firm plums, quince, cranberries and citrus fruits. Those less rich in pectin are apricots, blackberries, soft plums, raspberries, and loganberries. Fruits low in pectin are strawberries, cherries, pears, peaches, pineapple, rhubarb, melon and marrow, and extra pectin must be added to obtain well set jam made from these.

Acid helps to extract pectin from fruit, improves the flavour and colour of a jam and also helps to prevent crystallization. Fortunately, very acid fruits tend to be rich in pectin, whereas jams made with low pectin fruits usually need extra acid in the form of either lemon juice, citric or tartaric acid, or red currant or gooseberry juice (see recipes).

The right amount of sugar in a jam is vital to its setting and keeping properties: too little and a jam will ferment; too much and it will crystallize. So be sure to follow the amounts specified in recipes.

EQUIPMENT NEEDED

The first essential is a preserving pan or large saucepan, wide enough to allow for rapid boiling and evaporation. An aluminium or stainless steel pan with a heavy base to prevent sticking and burning, is the most suitable, though copper and brass pans can also be used as long as they are cleaned well. Never use an untinned iron or galvanized iron pan because acids in fruit attack the metal. Other items required are a long wooden spoon, a perforated spoon for skimming, a ladle, a thermometer capable of going up to 110°C/230°F, a heat-proof jug, a saucer, a funnel, scales, jam jars and covers (waxed discs and cellophane circles, together with rubber bands or string, or scrupulously clean plastic or metal airtight tops) and labels.

MAKING THE JAM

Choose ripe or slightly under-ripe, undamaged fruit (over-ripe fruit will contain less pectin), which is as fresh as possible. Rinse and drain well, then remove stalks, stems, stones, cores and peel, according to the fruit.

Softening the fruit: after its preparation, the fruit is cooked gently for some time before the sugar is added to soften the skins and help release the pectin. Sometimes spices and fruit peel and pips are tied in a muslin bag and cooked with the fruit to give additional flavour and pectin. Soft juicy fruits need no water added to the pan and a short cooking time, whereas harder fruits need just enough water added to prevent the fruit burning and a longer cooking time (between 30 and 45 minutes).

Pectin test: to check the pectin content of the softened fruit, place 1 × 5 ml spoon/1 teaspoon of the juice in a cup and leave to cool. Add 1 × 15 ml spoon/1 tablespoon methylated spirit and shake gently to combine. Leave for 1 minute, then carefully pour into another cup. If plenty of pectin is present, one jelly-like clot will form; if the pectin content is only moderate, the clot will be broken into 2 or 3 lumps; if very little pectin is present, the clot will be broken into lots of small pieces.

If the pectin content is low, continue to simmer the fruit to concentrate the juice by evaporation and test again. If the pectin content is still low add extra pectin in the form of juice from lemons, gooseberries, red currants or cooking apples. Alternatively, add commercial pectin (which is available from most chemists) following manufacturer's instructions.

When the fruit is soft the muslin bag is removed (if used) on to a saucer and the juice from it is squeezed back into the pan by pressing the bag with a wooden spoon and tilting the saucer over the pan.

Make sure the fruit skins are completely softened before adding the sugar because it has a hardening effect. Bring the fruit mixture to the boil, then simmer gently until it is reduced to a pulp. Add extra acid and pectin at this stage if necessary.

Adding the sugar: special preserving sugar crystals are available which reduce the scum formed and therefore give a clearer finish to a jam, but any kind of sugar can be used – cubes, granulated, caster, or brown – and half the quantity of sugar may be substituted by honey or syrup to give a different flavour.

However, the finished jam must contain 65 per cent sugar for it to keep satisfactorily. As a guide to quantities, add approximately 500 g/1 lb sugar for every 500 g/1 lb fruit (or 350 g/12 oz sugar for low pectin fruits and up to 750 g/1½ lb sugar for high pectin fruits). If the sugar is warmed gently in the oven before adding to the fruit, it dissolves more quickly and does not cool down the pulp, but it is not essential.

Stir the pulp over a gentle heat until the sugar is completely dissolved, then boil rapidly until setting point is reached. A large pan is essential as the jam will rise up in a froth and care must be taken not to let it boil over. After 2 to 3 minutes rapid boiling, begin testing the jam for its setting point (the point at which the jam will set on cooling).

When you think the jam is nearly set, turn off the heat while testing for setting point, so there is no risk of over-boiling which can weaken the setting property of a jam.

TESTING FOR SETTING POINT

This can be done in several ways, as follows:
Wooden spoon or flake test: dip a wooden spoon into the boiling jam, allow it to cool slightly so a thin skin forms, then pour it back into the pan. Setting point is reached when the drops of jam run off the tilted spoon in a large blob or form flakes before cleanly breaking away.
Saucer test: chill several saucers or plates in the refrigerator before you start to make the jam. When the jam is ready, put 1 × 5 ml spoon/1 teaspoon of jam on a cold saucer or plate and leave to cool slightly. Gently push your finger through the jam, the surface of which will wrinkle if the jam is at setting point.
Temperature: for this test you will need a thermometer that goes up to 110°C/230°F. Place the thermometer in a jug of hot water. Stir the jam, then dry the thermometer and place in the centre of the jam, but without letting it touch or rest on the bottom of the pan. Setting point is reached at a temperature of 104°C/220°F, providing sufficient acid and pectin are present. Return the thermometer to the hot water after the reading.

FILLING THE JARS

When setting point is reached, turn off the heat and immediately remove the scum from the surface of the jam with a wooden or perforated spoon. Pour the jam at once into clean, dry warm jars. Prepare these ahead: wash the jars thoroughly, rinse, drain and stand on a baking sheet in a cool oven (140°C/275°F, Gas Mark 1) while making the jam. Fill the jars right to the top with hot jam (on cooling the jam will shrink slightly in the jar). Use a heat-resistant jug or a ladle for pouring, with a funnel placed in the neck of the jar to prevent jam from spilling down the sides.

Whole fruit jams should be cooled slightly before potting, so they thicken a little and hold the fruit evenly through the jam, instead of rising to the top. Let a thin skin form on the surface; stir gently and then pour into the jars.

COVERING THE JARS

After filling, immediately place a small waxed disc (waxed side down) to cover the surface of the jam completely, and press gently to exclude all air. Cover the jars at once with cellophane, secured with a rubber band or string, or leave until cold, protected by a clean cloth or paper, before covering and securing. Airtight plastic or metal covers may also be used but these must be put on while the jam is still hot, so there is no chance of any mould growing during storage. Clean the jars and label them with the date and type of jam.

STORAGE OF JAM

Keep home-made jam in a cool, dry, dark, airy cupboard to avoid mould growth due to dampness, or shrinkage due to heat.

Strawberry and orange jam

Metric	Imperial
1 kg oranges	2 lb oranges
grated rind and juice of 2 lemons	grated rind and juice of 2 lemons
600 ml water	1 pint water
1 kg strawberries, hulled	2 lb strawberries, hulled
1½ kg preserving sugar	3 lb preserving sugar

Cooking time: about 1¼ hours

Wash the oranges and thinly peel the rind with a potato peeler. Cut the rind into thin strips. Cut the orange flesh into segments between the membrane, reserving the pith and pips.

Place the strips of orange rind in a saucepan together with the lemon rind and juice, and pour over the water. Tie the orange and lemon pith and pips in a muslin bag and add to the pan. Cover and bring to the boil. Simmer for 45 minutes or until the orange peel is softened.

Remove the muslin bag, squeezing the juice back into the pan. Add the orange segments and strawberries to the pan and return to the boil. Simmer for 10 minutes or until the fruit is soft but retains its shape. Add the sugar and heat gently, stirring until the sugar is dissolved. Bring to the boil, then boil rapidly until setting point is reached. Remove the scum. Cool slightly, stir, then pour into prepared jars. Cover and label.

Makes about 2¼ kg/5 lb

Currant berry jam; Strawberry jam; Strawberry and orange jam

Strawberry jam

Metric	Imperial
1¾ kg strawberries, hulled	4 lb strawberries, hulled
grated rind and juice of 3 large lemons	grated rind and juice of 3 large lemons
1½ kg preserving sugar	3½ lb preserving sugar

Cooking time: about 30 minutes

Place a few of the strawberries in a large pan and crush them with a wooden spoon. Add the remaining berries, together with the lemon rind and juice and heat gently to extract the fruit juice. Bring to the boil and simmer gently for 5 minutes.

Add the sugar and heat gently, stirring until the sugar is dissolved. Bring to the boil, then boil rapidly until setting point is reached. Remove the scum. Cool slightly, stir, then pour into prepared jars. Cover and label.

Makes about 2¾ kg/6 lb

Currant berry jam

Metric	Imperial
1 kg red currants	2 lb red currants
1 kg strawberries or raspberries, etc, hulled	2 lb strawberries or raspberries, etc, hulled
grated rind and juice of 2 oranges or lemons	grated rind and juice of 2 oranges or lemons
1¾ kg sugar	4 lb sugar

Cooking time: about 40 minutes

Strip the currants off the stalks by running a fork tine down each stalk. Place the currants and hulled berries in a large pan and add the rind and juice from the oranges or lemons. Heat gently to extract the juice, then simmer for 15 minutes.

Add the sugar and heat gently, stirring until the sugar is dissolved. Bring to the boil, then boil rapidly until setting point is reached. Remove the scum. Cool slightly, stir, then pour into prepared jars. Cover and label.

Makes about 3 kg/7 lb

Plum jam

Metric
1¾ kg cooking plums,
  washed and stalks
  removed
grated rind and juice of
  4 oranges
300 ml water
1¾ kg preserving
  sugar

Imperial
4 lb cooking plums,
  washed and stalks
  removed
grated rind and juice of
  4 oranges
½ pint water
4 lb preserving
  sugar

Cooking time: about 1¼ hours

Cut the plums in half, through to the stone, then twist to separate the two halves. Remove the stones and, if the plums are large, cut in half again. Place the prepared plums in a large pan. Add the orange rind and juice and the water. Bring to the boil and simmer gently for about 15 minutes.

Add the sugar and heat gently, stirring until the sugar is dissolved. Bring to the boil, then boil rapidly until setting point is reached. Remove the scum. Cool slightly, stir, then pour into prepared jars. Cover and label.

Makes about 2¾ kg/6 lb

Rhubarb jam

Metric
1 kg oranges
600 ml water
25 g root ginger,
  chopped
1 kg rhubarb
1½ kg preserving sugar
100 g chopped mixed
  peel

Imperial
2 lb oranges
1 pint water
1 oz root ginger,
  chopped
2 lb rhubarb
3 lb preserving sugar
4 oz chopped mixed
  peel

Cooking time: about 1¼ hours

Grate the rind from the oranges and reserve. Cut away the pith with a sharp knife and cut the flesh into segments between the membrane. Place the orange pith, membrane and pips in a saucepan. Pour in the water and add the root ginger. Cover the pan and bring to the boil, then reduce the heat and simmer for 30 minutes. Strain and reserve the liquid.

Wash and slice the rhubarb and place in a large pan with the orange rind and segments. Pour in the strained orange pith and ginger liquid. Bring to the boil and simmer for about 15 minutes.

Add the sugar and chopped mixed peel. Heat gently, stirring until the sugar is dissolved. Bring to the boil and boil rapidly until setting point is reached. Remove the scum. Cool slightly, stir, then pour into prepared jars. Cover and label.

Makes about 2½ kg/5¾ lb

Rhubarb and raspberry jam

Metric	Imperial
1 kg rhubarb, washed, trimmed and cut into 1 cm slices	2 lb rhubarb, washed, trimmed and cut into ½ in slices
150 ml water	¼ pint water
500 g raspberries, hulled	1 lb raspberries, hulled
grated rind and juice of 2 lemons	grated rind and juice of 2 lemons
1½ kg sugar	3 lb sugar

Cooking time: about 45 minutes

Place the rhubarb in a large pan and pour over the water. Heat gently and simmer for about 15 minutes or until the rhubarb is soft but still retains its shape. Add the raspberries, lemon rind and juice and return to simmering point.

Add the sugar and heat gently, stirring until the sugar is dissolved. Bring to the boil, then boil rapidly until setting point is reached. Remove the scum. Cool slightly, stir, then pour into prepared jars. Cover and label.

Makes about 2¼ kg/5 lb

Above: Raspberry and apple jam
Below: Rhubarb and raspberry jam;
Plum jam; Rhubarb jam

Raspberry and apple jam

Metric	Imperial
1½ kg cooking apples, peeled, cored (reserve peel and cores) and sliced	3 lb cooking apples, peeled, cored (reserve peel and cores) and sliced
grated rind and juice of 2 lemons, pith and pips reserved	grated rind and juice of 2 lemons, pith and pips reserved
600 ml water	1 pint water
1 kg raspberries, hulled	2 lb raspberries, hulled
1¾ kg preserving sugar	4 lb preserving sugar

Cooking time: about 45 minutes

Place the apples in a large pan, add the lemon rind and juice and pour over the water. Tie the apple cores, peel, lemon pith and pips in a muslin bag and add to the pan. Heat gently and bring to the boil. Simmer for about 15 minutes or until the apples are soft. Add the raspberries and simmer for about 15 minutes. Remove the muslin bag, squeezing the juice back into the pan. Add the sugar and heat gently, stirring until the sugar is dissolved. Bring to the boil, then boil rapidly until setting point is reached. Remove the scum. Cool slightly, stir, then pour into prepared jars. Cover and label.

Makes about 2¼ kg/5 lb

Fresh apricot jam

Metric	Imperial
1¾ kg fresh apricots	4 lb fresh apricots
600 ml water	1 pint water
grated rind and juice of 2 lemons	grated rind and juice of 2 lemons
1¾ kg sugar	4 lb sugar

Cooking time: about 45 minutes

Cut the apricots in half, through to the stone, then twist to separate the two halves and remove the stones. Crack open the stones with a hammer, take out the kernels, and remove their skins. Add the kernels to the apricot halves and place in a large pan. Pour over the water and add the lemon rind and juice. Heat gently and simmer for 10 to 15 minutes or until the apricots are soft but some pieces are still whole. Add the sugar and heat gently, stirring until the sugar is dissolved. Bring to the boil, then boil rapidly until setting point is reached. Remove the scum. Cool slightly, stir, then pour into prepared jars. Cover and label.
Makes about 2¾ kg/6 lb

Spiced cherry jam

Metric	Imperial
1¾ kg red cherries	4 lb red cherries
300 ml water	½ pint water
grated rind and juice of 750 g lemons, pith and pips reserved	grated rind and juice of 1½ lb lemons, pith and pips reserved
1 cinnamon stick	1 cinnamon stick
1 × 2.5 ml spoon cloves	½ teaspoon cloves
1¾ kg sugar	4 lb sugar

Cooking time: about 1 hour

Remove the stones from the cherries and reserve. Place the cherries in a large pan. Pour over the water and add the grated lemon rind and juice. Tie the cherry stones, lemon pith and pips, cinnamon and cloves in a muslin bag, then add this to the pan. Heat gently and simmer for about 30 to 45 minutes or until the cherries are soft.
Remove the muslin bag, squeezing the juice back into the pan. Add the sugar and heat gently, stirring until the sugar is dissolved. Bring to the boil, then boil rapidly until setting point is reached. Remove the scum. Cool slightly, stir, then pour into prepared jars. Cover and label.
Makes about 2¾ kg/6 lb

Queen of jams

Metric	Imperial
1½ kg peaches	3 lb peaches
grated rind and juice of 4 large lemons, pith and pips reserved	grated rind and juice of 4 large lemons, pith and pips reserved
450 ml water	¾ pint water
1 cinnamon stick	1 cinnamon stick
1 × 2.5 ml spoon cloves	½ teaspoon cloves
1 × 2.5 ml spoon allspice berries	½ teaspoon allspice berries
1½ kg preserving sugar	3 lb preserving sugar

Fresh apricot jam; Spiced cherry jam; Queen of jams

Cooking time: about 1 hour

Skin the peaches by steeping in boiling water for 10 to 20 seconds; drain and skin them. Cut in half, through to the stone, twist to separate the two halves and remove the stones. Slice the peaches and place in a large pan. Crack open the peach stones with a hammer, remove the skins from the kernels, then add kernels to the peaches. Add grated rind and juice of the lemons and pour over the water.

Tie the peach stones, lemon pith and pips, cinnamon, cloves and allspice in a muslin bag and add to the pan. Heat gently and simmer for about 30 minutes or until the peaches are soft but still retain their shape. Remove the muslin bag, squeezing the juice back into the pan. Add the sugar and heat gently, stirring until the sugar is dissolved. Bring to the boil, then boil rapidly until setting point is reached. Remove the scum. Cool slightly, stir, then pour into prepared jars. Cover and label.

Makes about 2¾ kg/6 lb

Spiced red currant and orange jam

Metric
1¾ kg red currants,
  stalks removed
grated rind and juice of
  6 oranges
1 cinnamon stick
1 × 5 ml spoon
  allspice berries
1 × 5 ml spoon cloves
2 kg sugar
100 g skinned
  hazelnuts, roughly
  chopped

Imperial
4 lb red currants,
  stalks removed
grated rind and juice of
  6 oranges
1 cinnamon stick
1 teaspoon allspice
  berries
1 teaspoon cloves
4½ lb sugar
4 oz skinned hazelnuts,
  roughly chopped

Cooking time: about 30 minutes

Place the currants in a large pan and add the orange rind and juice. Tie the cinnamon, allspice and cloves in a muslin bag and add to the pan. Heat gently and simmer for about 15 minutes or until the currants are soft.

Remove the muslin bag, squeezing the juice back into the pan. Add the sugar and the nuts and heat gently, stirring until the sugar is dissolved. Bring to the boil, then boil rapidly until setting point is reached. Remove the scum. Cool slightly, stir, then pour into prepared jars. Cover and label.

Makes about 3 kg/7 lb

Gooseberry and orange jam

Metric
1¾ kg gooseberries,
 topped and tailed
grated rind and juice of
 4 oranges
450 ml water
2 kg preserving sugar

Imperial
4 lb gooseberries,
 topped and tailed
grated rind and juice of
 4 oranges
¾ pint water
4½ lb preserving sugar

Cooking time: about 45 minutes

Place the gooseberries in a large pan. Add the orange rind and juice and the water. Bring to the boil and simmer for about 20 minutes or until the gooseberries are soft.
Add the sugar. Heat gently, stirring until the sugar is dissolved. Bring to the boil, then boil rapidly until setting point is reached. Remove the scum. Cool slightly, stir, then pour into prepared jars. Cover and label.
Makes about 3 kg/7 lb

Blackberry and pear jam

Metric
1 kg blackberries, picked
 over and washed
1½ kg cooking pears,
 peeled, cored (reserve
 peel and cores) and
 chopped
grated rind and juice of
 4 lemons, pith and
 pips reserved
3 sprigs of mint
 (optional)
1 cinnamon stick
1¾ kg sugar

Imperial
2 lb blackberries, picked
 over and washed
3 lb cooking pears,
 peeled, cored (reserve
 peel and cores) and
 chopped
grated rind and juice of
 4 lemons, pith and
 pips reserved
3 sprigs of mint
 (optional)
1 cinnamon stick
4 lb sugar

Cooking time: about 45 minutes

Place the blackberries and pears in a large pan together with the lemon rind and juice. Tie the reserved pear cores and peel, lemon pith and pips, mint, if used, and cinnamon stick in a muslin bag, and add to the pan. Heat gently to draw the juice out of the blackberries, then simmer for about 20 minutes or until the fruit is soft (if the pears are very hard, add a little water and cook longer).
Remove the muslin bag, squeezing the juice back into the pan. Add the sugar and heat gently, stirring until the sugar is dissolved. Bring to the boil, then boil rapidly until setting point is reached. Remove the scum. Cool slightly, stir, then pour into prepared jars. Cover and label.
Makes about 3 kg/7 lb

Spiced red currant and orange jam; Gooseberry and orange jam; Blackberry and pear jam

Pineapple jam; Apple ginger jam

Pineapple jam

Metric	Imperial
1 × 2¼ kg pineapple or 2 smaller ones	1 × 5 lb pineapple or 2 smaller ones
600 ml water	1 pint water
grated rind and juice of 4 lemons	grated rind and juice of 4 lemons
about 1½ kg sugar	about 3 lb sugar

Cooking time: about 1 hour

Cut off the ends of the pineapple, then cut it across into slices. Cut off the skin and 'eyes', and remove the hard central core. Weigh the pineapple flesh and calculate the amount of sugar needed – 500 g/1 lb sugar to 500 g/1 lb flesh.
Cut the pineapple flesh into small pieces and place in a large pan. Pour over the water and the lemon rind and juice. Heat gently and simmer for about 30 minutes or until the pineapple is soft.
Add the sugar and heat gently, stirring until the sugar is dissolved. Bring to the boil, then boil rapidly until setting point is reached. Remove the scum. Cool slightly, stir, then pour into prepared jars. Cover and label.
Makes about 1¾ kg/4 lb

Apple ginger jam

Metric	Imperial
1¾ kg cooking apples, peeled, cored (reserve peel and cores) and sliced	4 lb cooking apples, peeled, cored (reserve peel and cores) and sliced
900 ml water	1½ pints water
grated rind and juice of 2 lemons	grated rind and juice of 2 lemons
25 g root ginger, peeled and bruised or finely chopped	1 oz root ginger, peeled and bruised or finely chopped
100 g preserved ginger, finely chopped	4 oz preserved ginger, finely chopped
1½ kg sugar	3½ lb sugar

Cooking time: about 45 minutes

Place the apples in a large pan. Pour over the water and add the lemon rind. Tie the apple peel, cores, lemon pith and pips and root ginger (reserve the lemon juice for later) in a muslin bag and add to the pan. Simmer gently until the apples are soft.
Remove the muslin bag, squeezing the juice back into the pan. Add the preserved ginger (with 2 × 15 ml spoons/2 tablespoons of its syrup if available) and lemon juice. Add the sugar and heat gently, stirring until the sugar is dissolved. Bring to the boil, then boil rapidly until setting point is reached. Remove the scum. Cool slightly, stir, then pour into prepared jars. Cover and label.
Makes about 3 kg/7 lb

Somerset jam

Metric
1½ kg cooking apples, peeled, cored (reserve peel and cores) and sliced
1½ kg cooking pears, peeled, cored (reserve peel and cores) and sliced
1.2 litres cider
2 kg sugar

Imperial
3 lb cooking apples, peeled, cored (reserve peel and cores) and sliced
3 lb cooking pears, peeled, cored (reserve peel and cores) and sliced
2 pints cider
4¾ lb sugar

Cooking time: about 1 hour

Place the apples and pears in a large pan and pour over the cider. Tie the apple and pear peel and cores in a muslin bag and add to the pan. Heat gently and simmer for about 30 minutes or until the apples and pears are soft but some pieces are still whole.
Remove the muslin bag, squeezing the juice back into the pan. Add the sugar and heat gently, stirring until the sugar is dissolved. Bring to the boil, then boil rapidly until setting point is reached. Remove the scum. Cool slightly, stir, then pour into prepared jars. Cover and label.
Makes about 2¾ kg/6 lb

Somerset jam; Black currant and apple jam

Black currant and apple jam

Metric
1 kg black currants, stalks removed
1 kg cooking apples, peeled, cored and chopped
grated rind and juice of 2 lemons
900 ml water
2 kg preserving sugar

Imperial
2 lb black currants, stalks removed
2 lb cooking apples, peeled, cored and chopped
grated rind and juice of 2 lemons
1½ pints water
4¾ lb preserving sugar

Cooking time: about 1 hour

Place the prepared black currants and apples in a large pan. Add the lemon rind and juice and pour over the water. Simmer for 40 minutes or until soft.
Add the sugar and heat gently, stirring until the sugar is dissolved. Boil rapidly until setting point is reached. Remove the scum. Cool slightly, stir, then pour into prepared jars. Cover and label.
Makes about 3½ kg/8 lb

Dried apricot jam with oranges

Metric
1 kg dried apricots
2¼ litres water
grated rind and juice of
 3 oranges
grated rind and juice of
 1 lemon
1¾ kg sugar
100 g blanched split
 almonds

Imperial
2 lb dried apricots
4 pints water
grated rind and juice of
 3 oranges
grated rind and juice of
 1 lemon
4 lb sugar
4 oz blanched split
 almonds

Cooking time: about 1¼ hours

Place the dried apricots in a bowl, pour over the water, cover and leave overnight to soften the fruit. (Alternatively, to speed up the soaking, pour over boiling water to cover and leave for at least 2 hours.) Transfer the apricots with their soaking liquid to a large pan. Add the orange and lemon rinds and juice and bring to the boil. Simmer for about 45 to 60 minutes or until the apricots are very soft.

Add the sugar and almonds and heat gently, stirring until the sugar is dissolved. Bring to the boil, then boil rapidly until setting point is reached. Remove the scum. Cool slightly, stir, then pour into prepared jars. Cover and label.

Makes about 4 kg/9 lb

Dried fruit salad jam

Metric
1 kg mixed dried
 fruits (apricots,
 figs, prunes, apples,
 peaches, etc)
2¼ litres water
grated rind and juice of
 2 oranges
grated rind and juice of
 2 lemons
1¾ kg sugar

Imperial
2 lb mixed dried
 fruits (apricots, figs,
 prunes, apples,
 peaches, etc)
4 pints water
grated rind and juice of
 2 oranges
grated rind and juice of
 2 lemons
4 lb sugar

Cooking time: about 1¼ hours

Place the dried fruits in a bowl, pour over the water, cover and leave overnight to soften the fruit. (Alternatively, pour over boiling water to cover and leave for at least 2 hours.)

Discard any stones from the fruit, then transfer the fruit and liquid to a large pan. Add the orange and lemon rinds and juice and bring to the boil. Reduce the heat and simmer for about 45 to 60 minutes or until all the fruits are very soft.

Add the sugar and heat gently, stirring until the sugar is dissolved. Bring to the boil, then boil rapidly until setting point is reached. Remove the scum. Cool slightly, stir, then pour into prepared jars. Cover and label.

Makes about 4 kg/9 lb

Dried fruit salad jam;
Dried apricot jam with oranges

Harlequin jam

Harlequin jam

Cooking time: about 45 minutes

Place the gooseberries in a large pan and pour over the water. Heat gently and bring to the boil. Add the remaining fruits and simmer for about 20 minutes or until all the fruits are soft.

Add the sugar and heat gently, stirring until the sugar is dissolved. Bring to the boil, then boil rapidly until setting point is reached. Remove the scum. Cool slightly, stir, then pour into prepared jars. Cover and label.

Makes about 3 kg/7 lb

Metric	Imperial
500 g gooseberries, topped and tailed	1 lb gooseberries, topped and tailed
300 ml water	½ pint water
500 g red currants, stalks removed	1 lb red currants, stalks removed
500 g strawberries, hulled	1 lb strawberries, hulled
500 g raspberries, hulled	1 lb raspberries, hulled
1¾ kg sugar	4 lb sugar

FRUIT JELLIES

A fruit jelly is similar to a jam except that the cooked fruit is strained before boiling with sugar to give a sparkling clear preserve. The process takes longer than jams and the yield is smaller, so cheap and wild fruits are often used.

EQUIPMENT NEEDED

The same items as for jam making are needed, plus a jelly bag and a measuring jug. Special jelly bags made of a closely woven material like felt or flannel, are widely available; or make your own out of a square of the same material or a closely woven cotton or linen and sew tapes on all four corners, then hang the cloth between the legs of an upturned stool, or on a hook. Even a scalded teatowel can be used.

MAKING THE JELLY

Wash the fruit, remove any damaged or bruised parts and then weigh. It is not necessary to remove stalks, cores, peel or stones, etc, as these will be strained off later; however, large fruits should be cut into small pieces.

Gently simmer the prepared fruit in water until soft: juicy, soft fruits will need only a little water and a short cooking time whereas harder or tough-skinned fruits will need more water and a longer cooking time of between 30 to 60 minutes. This gentle cooking in water extracts the pectin and acid from the fruit. Test for pectin content as for jam, page 8.

Straining the fruit pulp: scald a jelly bag by pouring boiling water through and use while still damp. Place a bowl under the jelly bag and pour in the fruit pulp. Leave to drip for at least 2 hours or overnight, but do not leave longer than 24 hours. Squeezing the bag produces cloudy jelly.

Adding the sugar: measure the juice and, for every 600 ml/1 pint juice, add approximately 500 g/1 to 1¼ lb sugar; or for low pectin fruits add 350 g/12 oz sugar. Pour the juice into a large, clean pan and bring to the boil. Add the sugar and stir until dissolved, then boil rapidly for about 3 to 15 minutes or until setting point is reached (see testing the setting point of jams, page 10). When cold, a well set but not stiff jelly should form.

FILLING THE JARS

When setting point is reached, turn off the heat and remove the scum immediately. Last traces of scum can be removed by trailing a piece of absorbent paper over the surface, but do this quickly before the jelly starts to set. At once pour the jelly into dry warm jars (as for jam making, page 10), using a heat-resistant jug. (If small pieces of scum float to the top, quickly scoop them out.) Tilt the jars while pouring to prevent air bubbles forming. Cover and store jars as for jams.

Strawberry and gooseberry jelly

Metric	Imperial
1 kg gooseberries	*2 lb gooseberries*
1.2 litres water	*2 pints water*
1 kg strawberries	*2 lb strawberries*
approx 1 kg sugar	*approx 2 lb sugar*

Cooking time: about 1 hour

Rinse the gooseberries and place in a large pan with the water. Bring to the boil and simmer gently for 15 minutes.
Rinse the strawberries and add to the gooseberries in the pan. Simmer for about 15 minutes or until both gooseberries and strawberries are very soft.
Strain through a jelly bag and leave to drip for at least 2 hours or overnight. Measure the juice, pour into a large saucepan and bring to the boil. Add 500 g/ 1 lb sugar for every 600 ml/1 pint juice. Heat gently, stirring until the sugar is dissolved. Bring to the boil, then boil rapidly until setting point is reached. Remove the scum immediately and pour into prepared jars. Cover and label.
Makes about 1½ kg/3 lb

Raspberry and red currant jelly

Metric	Imperial
1 kg raspberries	*2 lb raspberries*
1 kg red currants	*2 lb red currants*
1 litre water	*1¾ pints water*
approx 1 kg sugar	*approx 2 lb sugar*

Cooking time: about 1 hour

Rinse the raspberries and red currants and place in a large pan. Pour over the water and heat gently to extract the juice, crushing the berries occasionally. Simmer gently for about 30 minutes or until the fruit is very soft.
Strain through a jelly bag and leave to drip for at least 2 hours or overnight. Measure the juice, pour into a large saucepan and bring to the boil. Add 500 g/1 lb sugar for every 600 ml/1 pint juice. Heat gently, stirring until the sugar is dissolved. Bring to the boil, then boil rapidly until setting point is reached. Remove the scum immediately and pour into prepared jars. Cover and label.
Makes about 1½ kg/3 lb

From left: Strawberry and gooseberry jelly; Raspberry and red currant jelly

23

Spiced apple jelly

Metric
2 kg cooking or
   crab apples
1¾ litres water
2 lemons, sliced
25 g root ginger,
   finely chopped or
   bruised
1 cinnamon stick
1 × 2.5 ml spoon cloves
approx 750 g sugar

Imperial
4½ lb cooking or
   crab apples
3 pints water
2 lemons, sliced
1 oz root ginger,
   finely chopped or
   bruised
1 cinnamon stick
½ teaspoon cloves
approx 1½ lb sugar

Cooking time: about 1½ hours

A few red berries may be added with the apples to give an attractive pale rose-coloured jelly. Also rose geranium leaves or lemon balm leaves may be added for extra flavour, and cider substituted for some of the water.

Wash the apples, cut up into pieces, discarding any bad bits, and place in a large pan. Pour over the water and add the lemons, ginger, cinnamon and cloves. Bring to the boil and simmer gently for 45 minutes to 1 hour or until the apples are very soft.
Strain through a jelly bag and leave to drip for at least 2 hours or overnight. Measure the juice, pour into a large saucepan and bring to the boil. Add 500 g/1 lb sugar for every 600 ml/1 pint juice. Heat gently, stirring until the sugar is dissolved. Bring to the boil, then boil rapidly until setting point is reached. Remove the scum immediately and pour into prepared jars. Cover and label.
Makes about 1½ kg/3 lb

Bramble jelly

Metric
1 kg blackberries
1 kg cooking apples
2 lemons, sliced
1.2 litres water
approx 1 kg sugar

Imperial
2 lb blackberries
2 lb cooking apples
2 lemons, sliced
2 pints water
approx 2 lb sugar

Cooking time: about 1 hour

Rinse the blackberries and place in a large pan. Wash the apples, cut up into pieces and add to the pan with the lemon slices. Pour over the water. Bring to the boil and simmer for 30 to 40 minutes or until the fruit is very soft.
Strain through a jelly bag and leave to drip for at least 2 hours or overnight. Measure the juice, pour into a large saucepan and bring to the boil. Add 500 g/1 lb sugar for every 600 ml/1 pint juice. Heat gently, stirring until the sugar is dissolved. Bring to the boil, then boil rapidly until setting point is reached. Remove the scum immediately and pour into prepared jars. Cover and label.
Makes about 1¾ kg/4 lb

Spiced apple jelly

From left: Bramble jelly; Black currant and orange jelly

Black currant and orange jelly

Metric	Imperial
1¾ kg black currants, leaves and coarse stalks removed	4 lb black currants, leaves and coarse stalks removed
1¾ litres water	3 pints water
4 oranges, sliced	4 oranges, sliced
4 sprigs of mint (optional)	4 sprigs of mint (optional)
approx 750 g sugar	approx 1½ lb sugar

Cooking time: about 1½ hours

Rinse the black currants and place in a large pan. Pour over the water and add the oranges and mint if used. Bring to the boil and simmer gently for about 1 hour, crushing the currants occasionally.

Strain through a jelly bag and leave to drip for at least 2 hours or overnight. Measure the juice, pour into a large pan and bring to the boil. Add 500 g/1 lb sugar for every 600 ml/1 pint juice. Heat gently, stirring until the sugar is dissolved. Bring to the boil, then boil rapidly until setting point is reached. Remove the scum immediately and pour into prepared jars. Cover and label.

Makes about 1½ kg/3 lb

From left: Spiced red currant jelly; Gooseberry jelly;
Spiced cranberry jelly; Damson and apple jelly

Damson and apple jelly

Metric	Imperial
1 kg damsons	*2 lb damsons*
1 kg apples	*2 lb apples*
1½ litres water	*2½ pints water*
approx 1 kg sugar	*approx 2 lb sugar*

Cooking time: about 1½ hours

Rinse the damsons and place, whole, in a large pan. Cut
the apples into pieces and add to the damsons in the
pan. Pour over the water and bring to the boil. Simmer
for 45 to 60 minutes or until the fruit is very soft.
Strain through a jelly bag and leave to drip for at least
2 hours or overnight. Measure the juice, pour into
a large pan and bring to the boil. Add 500 g/1 lb
sugar for every 600 ml/1 pint juice. Heat gently,
stirring until the sugar is dissolved. Bring to the
boil, then boil rapidly until setting point is reached.
Remove the scum immediately and pour into prepared
jars. Cover and label.
Makes about 1½ kg/3 lb

Spiced cranberry jelly

Metric	Imperial
1 kg cranberries	*2 lb cranberries*
1 kg cooking apples	*2 lb cooking apples*
4 oranges, sliced	*4 oranges, sliced*
1¾ litres water	*3 pints water*
1 cinnamon stick	*1 cinnamon stick*
2 mace blades	*2 mace blades*
1 × 2.5 ml spoon cloves	*½ teaspoon cloves*
1 × 2.5 ml spoon allspice berries	*½ teaspoon allspice berries*
approx 1 kg sugar	*approx 2 lb sugar*

Cooking time: about 1¼ hours

Rinse the cranberries and place in a large pan. Cut
the apples into pieces and add to the pan. Add the
oranges and pour over the water. Add the cinnamon,
mace, cloves and allspice and bring to the boil.
Simmer gently for about 45 minutes or until the fruit
is very soft.
Strain through a jelly bag and leave to drip for at
least 2 hours or overnight. Measure the juice, pour
into a large pan and bring to the boil. Add 500 g/1 lb
sugar for every 600 ml/1 pint juice. Heat gently,
stirring until the sugar is dissolved. Bring to the boil,
then boil rapidly until setting point is reached. Remove the scum immediately and pour into prepared
jars. Cover and label.
Makes about 1½ kg/3 lb

Gooseberry jelly

Metric	Imperial
1¾ kg gooseberries	4 lb gooseberries
1.2 litres water	2 pints water
approx 1 kg sugar	approx 2 lb sugar
4 large elderflowers	4 large elderflowers
(optional)	(optional)

Cooking time: about 1 hour

If elderflowers are available, rinse and tie them in a muslin bag; add this to the pan after the sugar has been dissolved, and remove before skimming. These flowers give a delicious 'muscat grape' flavour to the jelly. A few sprigs of mint can also be used to vary the flavour.

Rinse the gooseberries and place in a large pan. Pour over the water and bring to the boil. Simmer gently for 30 to 40 minutes or until very soft.
Strain through a jelly bag and leave to drip for at least 2 hours or overnight. Measure the juice, pour into a large pan and bring to the boil. Add 500 g/1 lb sugar for every 600 ml/1 pint of juice. Heat gently stirring until the sugar is dissolved. Add the elderflowers if using and bring to the boil. Boil rapidly until setting point is reached. Remove the flowers and scum immediately and pour into prepared jars. Cover and label.
Makes about 1½ kg/3 lb

Spiced red currant jelly

Metric	Imperial
1¾ kg red currants	4 lb red currants
1.2 litres water	2 pints water
1 × 5 ml spoon allspice berries	1 teaspoon allspice berries
1 × 2.5 ml spoon cloves	½ teaspoon cloves
2 large mace blades	2 large mace blades
1 cinnamon stick	1 cinnamon stick
approx 500 g sugar	approx 1¼ lb sugar

Cooking time: about 1 hour

Serve as jam or with roast lamb.

Rinse the red currants and place in a large pan. Pour over the water and add the allspice, cloves, mace and cinnamon. Bring to the boil and simmer gently for about 40 minutes or until very soft, crushing the currants occasionally.
Strain through a jelly bag, and leave to drip for at least 2 hours or overnight. Measure the juice, pour into a large pan and bring to the boil. Add 500 g/1 lb sugar for every 600 ml/1 pint juice. Heat gently, stirring until the sugar is dissolved. Bring to the boil, then boil rapidly until setting point is reached. Remove the scum immediately and pour into prepared jars. Cover and label.
Makes about 1 kg/2 lb

Apricot jelly

Metric
1¾ kg fresh apricots
1.2 litres water
2 lemons, sliced
approx 1 kg sugar

Imperial
4 lb fresh apricots
2 pints water
2 lemons, sliced
approx 2 lb sugar

Cooking time: about 1½ hours

Place the whole apricots in a large pan with the water and lemons, bring to the boil and simmer for about 30 minutes. After 20 minutes crush with a wooden spoon to release the stones, then continue to cook until very soft.

Strain through a jelly bag and leave to drip for at least 2 hours or overnight. Measure the juice, pour into a large pan and bring to the boil. Add 500 g/1 lb sugar for every 600 ml/1 pint juice. Heat gently, stirring until the sugar is dissolved, then bring to the boil and boil rapidly until setting point is reached. Remove the scum immediately and pour into prepared jars. Cover and label.

Makes about 1¼ kg/2½ lb

Gingered rhubarb jelly; Apricot jelly

Medley jelly

Gingered rhubarb jelly

Metric	Imperial
1½ kg rhubarb, chopped	3 lb rhubarb, chopped
500 g red currants	1 lb red currants
4 oranges, sliced	4 oranges, sliced
25 g root ginger, finely chopped or bruised	1 oz root ginger, finely chopped or bruised
1.2 litres water	2 pints water
approx 1¼ kg sugar	approx 2½ lb sugar

Cooking time: about 1 hour

Rinse the rhubarb and currants and place in a large pan. Add the oranges and ginger and pour over the water. Bring to the boil and simmer gently for about 30 minutes or until the fruit is very soft.
Strain through a jelly bag and leave to drip for at least 2 hours or overnight. Measure the juice, pour into a large pan and bring to the boil. Add 500 g/1 lb sugar for every 600 ml/1 pint juice. Heat gently, stirring until the sugar is dissolved. Bring to the boil, then boil rapidly until setting point is reached. Remove the scum immediately and pour into prepared jars. Cover and label.
Makes about 1¾ kg/4 lb

Medley jelly

Metric	Imperial
500 g gooseberries	1 lb gooseberries
500 g strawberries or raspberries	1 lb strawberries or raspberries
500 g red currants	1 lb red currants
500 g rhubarb, chopped	1 lb rhubarb, chopped
1.2 litres water	2 pints water
approx 1 kg sugar	approx 2 lb sugar

Cooking time: about 1¼ hours

Other fruits may be substituted, e.g. cooking apples, plums, etc, but it is best to have a balance of high and low pectin fruits.

Rinse the fruits and place in a large pan. Pour over the water and bring to the boil. Simmer gently for about 45 minutes or until all the fruits are very soft.
Strain through a jelly bag and leave to drip for at least 2 hours or overnight. Measure the juice, pour into a large pan and bring to the boil. Add 500 g/1 lb sugar for every 600 ml/1 pint juice. Heat gently, stirring until the sugar is dissolved. Bring to the boil, then boil rapidly until setting point is reached. Remove any scum immediately and pour into prepared jars. Cover and label.
Makes about 1½ kg/3 lb

Orange and thyme jelly

Orange and thyme jelly

Metric
1 kg oranges
1 kg lemons
2 litres water
approx 750 g sugar
4 × 15 ml spoons
  fresh thyme leaves

Imperial
2 lb oranges
2 lb lemons
3½ pints water
approx 1½ lb sugar
4 tablespoons
  fresh thyme leaves

Cooking time: about 1½ hours

Wash the oranges and lemons and cut up into small pieces (slice, then cut the slices into halves or quarters). Place the orange and lemon pieces in a large pan and pour over the water. Bring to the boil and simmer for about 1 hour or until the fruit is soft.
Strain through a jelly bag and leave to drip for at least 2 hours or overnight. Measure the juice, pour into a large pan and bring to the boil. Add 500 g/1 lb sugar for every 600 ml/1 pint juice. Heat gently, stirring until the sugar is dissolved. Bring to the boil, then boil rapidly until setting point is reached. Remove any scum immediately and stir in the thyme leaves. Cool slightly until a thin skin forms on the surface, stir gently and pour into prepared jars.
Cover and label.
Makes about 1½ kg/3 lb

Tomato and herb jelly

Metric
1¾ kg tomatoes
300 ml water
300 ml malt vinegar
2 lemons, sliced
bunch of fresh herbs
  (rosemary, thyme,
  mint, parsley, bay leaf)
approx 1 kg sugar

Imperial
4 lb tomatoes
½ pint water
½ pint malt vinegar
2 lemons, sliced
bunch of fresh herbs,
  (rosemary, thyme,
  mint, parsley, bay leaf)
approx 2 lb sugar

Cooking time: about 1 hour

Serve with meat, especially lamb. Half the quantity of tomatoes may be replaced by chopped cooking apples. Wash the tomatoes, cut into quarters and place in a large pan. Pour over the water and vinegar and add the lemons. Add the herbs, about 12 sprigs altogether (use just one herb or a mixture of herbs as desired). Bring to the boil and simmer gently for about 30 minutes or until the tomatoes are very soft. Strain through a jelly bag and leave to drip for at least 2 hours or overnight. Measure the juice, pour into a large pan and bring to the boil. Add 500 g/1 lb sugar for every 600 ml/1 pint juice. Heat gently, stirring until the sugar is dissolved. Bring to the boil, then boil rapidly until setting point is reached. Remove any scum immediately and pour into prepared jars. (If liked place a sprig of fresh herbs in the jar before pouring in the jelly to vary the flavour and appearance.) Cover and label.
Makes about 1½ kg/3 lb

Mint jelly

Metric
1½ kg cooking apples
1.2 litres water
600 ml wine vinegar
bunch of fresh mint
approx 750 g sugar
few drops green food
  colouring (optional)

Imperial
3 lb cooking apples
2 pints water
1 pint wine vinegar
bunch of fresh mint
approx 1½ lb sugar
few drops green food
  colouring (optional)

Cooking time: about 1¼ hours

Wash the apples, cut up into pieces and place in a large pan. Pour over the water and vinegar. Strip off the best leaves from the mint and reserve to make about 3 to 4×15 ml spoons/3 to 4 tablespoons chopped mint. Add the remaining mint, with stalks, to the pan. Bring to the boil and simmer gently for about 45 minutes or until the apples are very soft.
Strain through a jelly bag and leave to drip for at least 2 hours or overnight. Measure the juice, pour into a large pan and bring to the boil. Add 500 g/1 lb sugar for every 600 ml/1 pint juice. Heat gently, stirring until the sugar is dissolved. Bring to the boil, then boil rapidly until setting point is reached. Remove any scum immediately and stir in the reserved chopped mint. Cool slightly until a thin skin forms on the surface, stir gently and pour into prepared jars. Cover and label.
Makes about 1½ kg/3 lb

Variations:
Other fresh herbs can be substituted for mint, e.g. thyme, sage, parsley and rosemary. Serve with roast meats – rosemary jelly with lamb, thyme jelly with poultry, sage jelly with pork and parsley jelly with cold gammon.

Tomato and herb jelly; Mint jelly and variations

MARMALADES

Marmalade is a jam made from citrus fruits and is made in much the same way as jam, except that the peel is included during the boiling with sugar. As citrus peel requires longer cooking to soften it, so more water is required than for jam-making. Marmalade can vary from a thick, chunky consistency to a clear jelly containing thin shreds of peel. It traditionally appears at the British breakfast table, but can also be used for flavouring sauces, puddings and cakes.

Citrus fruits are oranges, lemons, limes and grapefruit as well as a few other related fruits like tangerines. All these give an outstanding variety of delicious flavours, either used singly or mixed together. The bitter Seville oranges are the most popular for marmalade because of their flavour and appearance. The peel of sweet oranges gives marmalade a rather cloudy appearance, and the pith does not turn as translucent as that of Seville oranges. Unfortunately, Seville oranges have a very short season, lasting from early January to about the end of February, when they are usually in good supply, so they may be frozen whole or bottled for use later in the year.

All citrus fruits are high in pectin. This is contained principally in the pith and pips and is most easily extracted by tying them in a muslin bag, which is then added to the fruit in the pan. The naturally high acid content of citrus fruits speeds up the process of making the pectin soluble. However, more acid is added in some marmalade recipes (see following pages). Amounts vary but the purpose is to bring up the level of the acid to a point that will ensure a good set.

Testing for the pectin content is carried out exactly as for jams by means of methylated spirit (see page 8); however, there is less necessity to test marmalade because the pectin content of citrus fruits is more reliable than other fruits.

Preparing the fruit for marmalade making takes a long time and it may be more convenient to prepare the fruit one day and leave it to soak in the water until the next day; however this overnight soaking does not particularly improve the quality of the finished marmalade. But whether the fruit peel is shredded or left in chunks, it is important that the cutting of both fruit and peel is uniform for best results.

Before any sugar can be added, the fruit needs fairly prolonged cooking to soften the peel and reduce the flesh to a pulp. As a rule, 1 to 1½ hours should be adequate for this softening-up process and driving off the excess water.

The boiling time after sugar is added should be no longer than 15 to 20 minutes for a good set. Unnecessary boiling over the specified time will result in dark-looking and badly set marmalade.

ACHIEVING A CLEAR OR CHUNKY MARMALADE

There are several different ways of preparing and softening the fruit resulting in a different consistency and appearance of the marmalade.

Choose whichever method is most convenient to you and which type of marmalade you prefer.

Method 1: this is the easiest method and used in most of the following recipes giving a thick, chunky marmalade.

Wash the fruit, cut in half and squeeze out the juice, reserving the pips. Slice the peel, without removing the pith, into shreds – it may be easier to cut the squeezed orange halves into half again before shredding. If making large quantities, it is easier to cut the fruit into halves or quarters depending on size: squeeze out the juice using a compressor type juice squeezer which is operated like a large garlic press, and the juice collects in a container below. This also flattens the peels which are then easier to shred. Cut the shreds of peel thickly or thinly as desired in the finished marmalade.

Place the fruit juice and shredded peel in a large pan with the pips tied in a muslin bag. Pour over the measured quantity of water and bring to the boil. Reduce the heat and simmer for 1 to 2 hours until the peel is very soft and disintegrates when squeezed between the fingers. Remove the muslin bag, squeezing the juice back into the pan.

Add the sugar and stir over a low heat until the sugar dissolves. Boil rapidly until setting point is reached.

Method 2: the pith is not included in the finished marmalade and is particularly used with thick skinned fruit to give a finer texture.

Wash the fruit. Thinly pare off the rind using a potato peeler so that the pith is left on the fruit. Cut the peeled rind into shreds. Either cut the fruit in half and squeeze out the juice, or cut off the pith with a sharp knife and slice or coarsely chop the flesh. Place the shredded rind in a large pan with the fruit juice of the chopped flesh. Tie the pith and pips in a muslin bag and add to the pan. Pour in the measured quantity of water and bring to the boil. Reduce the heat and simmer for 1 to $1\frac{1}{4}$ hours until the rind is very soft (this will not take as long as Method 1). Add the sugar and continue as for Method 1.

Alternatively, place the shredded peel in a pan with half the water and simmer for 1 to $1\frac{1}{2}$ hours until soft. Coarsely chop the rest of the fruit with the pith and place in another pan with the remaining water. Cover and simmer for 1 to $1\frac{1}{2}$ hours until softened. Strain through a colander to remove pips and coarse tissue or rub through a sieve to give a thicker marmalade. Add the strained pulp to the peel and water. Add the sugar and continue as for Method 1.

Method 3: the fruit is cooked whole, then cut up before adding the sugar, but it is rather a messy operation!

Wash the fruit and place in a large pan. Cover and bring to the boil. Reduce the heat and simmer for $1\frac{1}{2}$ to 2 hours until the peel is very soft. (Alternatively place the fruit in a large casserole, pour on measured boiling water, cover and cook in a slow oven for 4 to 5 hours until softened.) Remove the fruit with a slotted spoon to a board. Cut up the fruit, thickly or thinly as desired, using a knife and fork. Remove the pips and add to the water (they can be tied in a muslin bag) and boil for 5 minutes to extract the remaining pectin. Remove the pips. Add the sliced fruit with any juice to the boiling water. Add the sugar and continue as for Method 1.

Pressure cooker: this is ideal for saving time and fuel for the usually long process of softening the fruit.

Prepare the fruit by Methods 1, 2 or 3 and place in the pressure cooker, without the trivet, with half the amount of water stated in the recipe. Bring to H (15 lb) pressure and cook for 10 to 20 minutes depending on preparation of fruit. Reduce pressure slowly and

remove the lid. Add sugar and continue as for Method 1. Do not bring to pressure again.

Many pressure cookers will not make more than $2\frac{1}{4}$ kg/5 lb marmalade at once, so follow the manufacturer's instructions.

COVERING AND STORING
Skim the marmalade as soon as it reaches setting point to clear it of scum, then cool it a little in the pan until a thin skin starts to form so the peel is suspended evenly and will not rise to the top when the marmalade is poured into jars. Stir briefly, then pour into clean, warm, *not* hot, jars. Cover at once with waxed circles (see jam-making, page 10), wipe clean and add lids or cellophane covers, usually when the marmalade is cold (see jam-making, page 10). Label and store in a cool, dark, airy place.

Equipment needed: the same items are required as for jam-making, plus a pressure cooker, muslin, and a lemon squeezer.

Mincer/liquidizer: instead of shredding the fruit by hand it may be minced or liquidized with some of the measured water. This does not give such a good consistency to the marmalade, but if making large quantities half of the fruit may be minced or liquidized and added to the hand-cut fruit.

Seville orange marmalade; Dark Seville marmalade

Seville orange marmalade

Metric
1½ kg Seville oranges
3½ litres water
juice of 2 lemons, or
*   1 × 5 ml spoon citric*
*   or tartaric acid*
2¾ kg preserving sugar

Imperial
3 lb Seville oranges
6 pints water
juice of 2 lemons, or
*   1 teaspoon citric or*
*   tartaric acid*
6 lb preserving sugar

Cooking time: about 2 hours

Wash the oranges and remove the stalks if necessary. Cut the oranges in half, squeeze out the juice and pour into a large pan. Tie the pips in a piece of muslin and add to the juice in the pan. Slice the orange peel and pith into thick or thin shreds, then add to the pan.
Pour the water into the pan with the lemon or acid, and bring to the boil. Reduce the heat and simmer for 1½ hours or until the peel is very soft. It should disintegrate when squeezed between the fingers. Remove the muslin bag, squeezing the juice back into the pan.
Add the sugar and stir over a low heat until it is dissolved. Boil rapidly until setting point is reached. Remove the scum. Allow to cool slightly before pouring into prepared jars. Wipe them clean and cover (see page 10), label and store.
Makes about 4½ kg/10 lb

Dark Seville marmalade

Metric
1½ kg Seville oranges
2 lemons
3½ litres water
2¾ kg soft brown sugar,
*   or white sugar with 2*
*   × 15 ml spoons black*
*   treacle*

Imperial
3 lb Seville oranges
2 lemons
6 pints water
6 lb soft brown sugar,
*   or white sugar with 2*
*   tablespoons black*
*   treacle*

Cooking time: about 2 hours

Wash the oranges and lemons, then cut in half. Squeeze out the juice and pour into a large pan. Tie the pips in a piece of muslin and add to the juice in the pan. Slice the orange and lemon peels into thick shreds without removing the pith, then add to the pan.
Pour the water into the pan and bring to the boil. Reduce the heat and simmer for about 1½ hours or until the peel is very soft. Remove the muslin bag, squeezing the juice back into the pan.
Add the sugar and stir over a low heat until dissolved. Boil rapidly until setting point is reached. Remove the scum. Allow to cool slightly before pouring into prepared jars. Wipe them clean and cover (see page 10), label and store.
Makes about 4½ kg/10 lb

Above: ripe or slightly under-ripe Seville oranges may be used in marmalade making.
Right: Boiling Seville orange marmalade

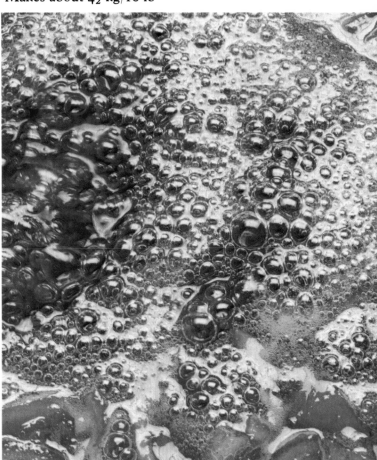

Citrus marmalade; Grapefruit marmalade

Citrus marmalade

Metric	Imperial
1½ kg mixed citrus fruit (about 2 medium grapefruit, 2 medium oranges, 4 medium lemons)	3 lb mixed citrus fruit (about 2 medium grapefruit, 2 medium oranges, 4 medium lemons)
3½ litres water	6 pints water
2¾ kg sugar	6 lb sugar

Cooking time: about 2 hours

Wash the citrus fruits and cut in half. Squeeze out the juice and pour into a large pan. Tie the pips in a piece of muslin and add to the juice in the pan. Cut the orange and lemon peels into half again, and the grapefruit peel into quarters. Slice the peels into thick or thin shreds, without removing the pith, and add to the pan.

Pour the water into the pan and bring to the boil. Reduce the heat, then simmer for 1½ hours or until the peel is very soft. Remove the muslin bag, squeezing the juice back into the pan.

Add the sugar and stir over a low heat until dissolved. Boil rapidly until setting point is reached. Remove the scum. Allow to cool slightly before pouring into prepared jars. Wipe them clean and cover (see page 10), label and store.

Makes about 4½ kg/10 lb

Grapefruit marmalade

Metric	Imperial
1 kg grapefruit	2 lb grapefruit
500 g lemons	1 lb lemons
3½ litres water	6 pints water
2¾ kg sugar	6 lb sugar

Cooking time: about 1½ hours

Wash the grapefruit and lemons. Thinly pare off the rind with a potato peeler and then cut the rind into thin strips and place in a large pan. Cut the pith from the fruit with a sharp knife. Slice the fruit and add it to the pan with any juice. Tie the pips and pith in a large piece of muslin and add to the pan.

Pour the water into the pan and bring to the boil. Reduce the heat, then simmer for about 1 hour or until the fruit is very soft. Remove the muslin bag, squeezing the juice back into the pan.

Add the sugar and stir over a low heat until dissolved. Boil rapidly until setting point is reached. Remove the scum. Allow to cool slightly before pouring into prepared jars. Wipe them clean and cover (see page 10), label and store.

Makes about 4½ kg/10 lb

Lime marmalade; Tangerine marmalade

Lime marmalade

Metric	Imperial
1½ kg limes	3 lb limes
3½ litres water	6 pints water
2¾ kg sugar	6 lb sugar

Cooking time: about 2 hours

Wash the limes and cut in half. Squeeze out the juice and pour into a large pan. Slice the lime peel into thin shreds without removing the pith, then add to the pan. Tie any pips in a muslin bag and add to the pan. Pour the water into the pan and bring to the boil. Reduce the heat, then simmer for 1½ hours or until the lime peel is very soft. Remove the muslin bag, squeezing the juice back into the pan.

Add the sugar and stir over a low heat until dissolved. Boil rapidly until setting point is reached. Remove the scum. Allow to cool slightly before pouring into pre-prepared jars. Wipe them clean and cover (see page 10), label and store.

Makes about 4½ kg/10 lb

Variation:

For a clearer marmalade with shreds of peel, prepare the limes by paring the rind with a potato peeler and cutting into thin shreds. Slice the lime flesh, placing the pith and pips in a muslin bag.

Tangerine marmalade

Metric	Imperial
1 kg tangerines	2 lb tangerines
500 g lemons	1 lb lemons
3½ litres water	6 pints water
2¾ kg sugar	6 lb sugar

Cooking time: about 1½ hours

Wash the tangerines and lemons, then cut in half. Squeeze out the juice and pour into a large pan. Tie the pips in a piece of muslin and add to the juice in the pan. Slice the tangerine and lemon peels into shreds without removing the pith and add to the pan. Pour the water into the pan and bring to the boil. Reduce the heat, then simmer for 1½ hours or until the peel is very soft. Remove the muslin bag, squeezing the juice back into the pan.

Add the sugar and stir over a low heat until dissolved. Boil rapidly until setting point is reached. Remove the scum. Allow to cool slightly before pouring into pre-pared jars. Wipe them clean and cover (see page 10), label and store.

Makes about 4½ kg/10 lb

Lemon and apple marmalade

Metric
750 g lemons
1¼ kg cooking apples
3½ litres water
1¾ kg sugar
1 kg honey

Imperial
1½ lb lemons
2½ lb cooking apples
6 pints water
4 lb sugar
2 lb honey

Cooking time: about 2 hours

Wash the lemons and cut in half. Squeeze out the juice, reserving the pips and pour into a large pan. Slice the lemon peel into thin shreds without removing the pith and add to the pan.

Peel, core and quarter the apples. Slice the apples and add to the pan. Tie the peels, cores and pips in a piece of muslin and add to the fruit in the pan.

Pour the water into the pan and bring to the boil. Reduce the heat, then simmer for 1½ hours or until the lemon peel is very soft. Remove the muslin bag, squeezing the juice back into the pan.

Add the sugar and honey and stir over a low heat until dissolved. Boil rapidly until setting point is reached. Remove the scum. Allow to cool slightly before pouring into prepared jars. Wipe them clean and cover (see page 10), label and store.

Makes about 4½ kg/10 lb

Autumn marmalade

Metric
500 g oranges
500 g lemons
500 g cooking apples
500 g pears
3½ litres water
2¾ kg sugar

Imperial
1 lb oranges
1 lb lemons
1 lb cooking apples
1 lb pears
6 pints water
6 lb sugar

Cooking time: about 2 hours

Wash the oranges and lemons and cut in half. Squeeze out the juice and pour into a large pan, reserving the pips. Slice the oranges and lemons into shreds, without removing the pith, and add to the pan.

Peel, quarter and core the apples and pears. Slice the apple and pear flesh and add to the pan. Tie all the peels, cores and pips in a large piece of muslin and add to the fruit in the pan.

Pour the water into the pan and bring to the boil. Reduce the heat, then simmer for 1½ hours until the peel is very soft. Remove the muslin bag, squeezing the juice back into the pan.

Add the sugar and stir over a low heat until dissolved. Boil rapidly until setting point is reached. Remove the scum. Allow to cool slightly before pouring into prepared jars. Wipe them clean and cover (see page 10), label and store.

Makes about 4½ kg/10 lb

Lemon and apple marmalade; Autumn marmalade

Apricot marmalade

Apricot marmalade

Metric
500 g oranges
500 g lemons
350 g dried apricots
3½ litres water
2¾ kg sugar

Imperial
1 lb oranges
1 lb lemons
12 oz dried apricots
6 pints water
6 lb sugar

Cooking time: about 2 hours

Wash the oranges and lemons and cut in half. Squeeze out the juice and pour into a large pan. Tie the pips in a piece of muslin and add to the juice in the pan. Slice the orange and lemon peels into shreds without removing the pith, and add to the pan.

Chop or shred the apricots (if they are tough this is easier with scissors) and add to the pan. Pour the water into the pan and bring to the boil. Reduce the heat, then simmer for 1½ hours or until the fruit is very soft. Remove the muslin bag, squeezing the juice back into the pan.

Add the sugar and stir over a low heat until dissolved. Boil rapidly until setting point is reached. Remove the scum. Allow to cool slightly before pouring into prepared jars. Wipe them clean and cover (see page 10), label and store.

Makes about 4½ kg/10 lb

Carrot and orange marmalade

Metric	Imperial
500 g carrots, peeled	*1 lb carrots, peeled*
500 g oranges	*1 lb oranges*
500 g lemons	*1 lb lemons*
3½ litres water	*6 pints water*
2¾ kg sugar	*6 lb sugar*

Cooking time: about 2 hours

Cut the carrots into matchstick strips and place in a large pan. Wash the oranges and lemons and cut in half. Squeeze the juice and add to the carrots in the pan. Slice the orange and lemon peel into thin shreds without removing the pith, then add to the pan. Tie the pips in a muslin bag and add to the pan.

Pour the water into the pan and bring to the boil. Reduce the heat, then simmer for 1½ hours or until the peel is very soft. Remove the muslin bag, squeezing the juice back into the pan.

Add the sugar and stir over a low heat until dissolved. Boil rapidly until the setting point is reached. Remove the scum. Allow to cool before pouring into prepared jars. Wipe them clean and cover (see page 10), label and store.

Makes about 4½ kg/10 lb

Orange peel and sultana marmalade

Metric	Imperial
350 g orange peel	*12 oz orange peel*
500 g lemons	*1 lb lemons*
350 g sultanas	*12 oz sultanas*
100 g mixed peel	*4 oz mixed peel*
3½ litres water	*6 pints water*
2¾ kg white sugar	*6 lb white sugar*

Cooking time: about 2 hours

You will need about 1 kg/2 lb (8 small) oranges for this quantity of peel.

Cut the peel and pith from the oranges. The orange flesh may be used for something else. Cut the peel with the pith into shreds and place in a large pan.

Cut the lemons in half, squeeze out the juice and add to the pan. Cut the lemon peel into shreds and add to the pan. Tie the pips in a muslin bag and add to the pan.

Add the sultanas and water and bring to the boil. Reduce the heat, then simmer for 1½ hours or until the peel is very soft. Remove the muslin bag, squeezing the juice back into the pan. Add the sugar and stir over a low heat until dissolved. Boil rapidly until setting point is reached. Remove the scum. Allow to cool slightly before pouring into prepared jars.

Wipe them clean and cover (see page 10), label and store.

Makes about 4½ kg/10 lb

Carrot and orange marmalade;
Orange peel and sultana marmalade

Ginger marmalade

Metric	Imperial
750 g oranges, sweet or Seville	1½ lb oranges, sweet or Seville
500 g lemons	1 lb lemons
25 g root ginger, peeled and chopped	1 oz root ginger, peeled and chopped
3½ litres water	6 pints water
2¾ kg sugar	6 lb sugar
225 g preserved ginger, finely chopped	8 oz preserved ginger, finely chopped

Cooking time: about 2 hours

Wash the oranges and lemons and cut in half. Squeeze the juice and pour into a large pan. Tie the pips with the root ginger in a muslin bag and add to the pan. Slice the orange and lemon peel into thin shreds, without removing the pith, and add to the pan. Pour the water into the pan and bring to the boil. Reduce the heat, then simmer for 1½ hours or until the fruit is very soft. Remove the muslin bag, squeezing the juice back into the pan.

Add the sugar and chopped ginger, and stir over a low heat until the sugar is dissolved. Boil rapidly until the setting point is reached. Remove the scum. Allow to cool slightly before pouring into prepared jars. Wipe them clean and cover (see page 10), label and store.
Makes about 4½ kg/10 lb

Jelly marmalade

Metric	Imperial
1½ kg citrus fruit (Seville or sweet oranges, lemons, limes, grapefruit)	3 lb citrus fruit (Seville or sweet oranges, lemons, limes, grapefruit)
3½ litres water	6 pints water
juice of 3 lemons, or 2 × 5 ml spoons citric or tartaric acid	juice of 3 lemons, or 2 teaspoons citric or tartaric acid

Cooking time: about 2 hours

Wash the fruit. Thinly peel off the rind without the pith, using a potato peeler. Shred the rind thinly and tie loosely in a muslin bag and place in a large pan. Coarsely cut up the rest of the fruit and add to the pan, including the pith and pips. Pour the water over with the lemon juice or acid, cover the pan and bring to the boil. Reduce the heat, then simmer for 1½ hours or until the peel is very soft.
Remove the muslin bag, squeezing the juice back into the pan. Remove the rind from the bag and reserve. Pour the cooked fruit and liquid into a scalded jelly bag over a bowl. Leave to drip, without squeezing, for at least 2 hours or until all the liquid has dripped through.
Measure the juice and for each 600 ml/1 pint of liquid add 500 g/1 lb sugar. Place the measured liquid and sugar into a clean pan. Stir over a low heat until the sugar is dissolved. Add the cooked shreds and boil rapidly until setting point is reached. Remove the scum. Allow to cool slightly before pouring into prepared jars. Wipe them clean and cover (see page 10), label and store.
Makes about 2 kg/4½ lb

Ginger marmalade; Jelly marmalade

CONSERVES

Conserves are a preserve of whole or chopped pieces of fruit suspended in a thick syrup. They do not set as firmly as jam and may be served as a dessert.

MAKING A CONSERVE

The prepared fruit is layered with sugar overnight. This toughens the skins of the fruit so that they will retain their shape and also extracts the juices so no extra water is necessary. The fruit is then simmered with the juice, sugar and acid until a thick syrup is formed; if the fruit is very juicy, the juice extracted and the sugar are boiled to a syrup before the fruit is added to the pan. The conserves are cooled until the fruit remains evenly suspended in the syrup before pouring into jars. Use the same equipment as for jam-making (see page 8) and cover and store in the same way. Conserves do not keep as well as jams so the jars should be checked regularly.

Strawberry and melon conserve; Peach and raspberry conserve

Strawberry and melon conserve

Metric
1½ kg strawberries, hulled
1 large melon (about 1¾ kg), peel and seeds removed and cut into 1 cm cubes
1¾ kg sugar
grated rind and juice of 4 lemons

Imperial
3 lb strawberries, hulled
1 large melon (about 4 lb), peel and seeds removed and cut into ½ inch cubes
4 lb sugar
grated rind and juice of 4 lemons

Cooking time: about 45 minutes

Layer the strawberries, melon cubes and sugar in a bowl. Cover and leave for 24 hours to firm the fruit and extract the juice. Strain off and reserve the fruit. Transfer the juice and sugar to a large pan. Heat gently, stirring until the sugar is dissolved, then bring to the boil. Boil rapidly to reduce the juice by half, for about 30 minutes or until it is a thick syrup. Add the fruit, lemon rind and juice and simmer gently for 5 minutes or until the fruit is tender but still retains its shape. Cool completely before pouring into prepared jars. Cover as for jam (see page 10).
Makes about 2¾ kg/6 lb

Peach and raspberry conserve

Metric
1 kg sugar
300 ml dry white wine or water
grated rind and juice of 1 lemon
1 kg peaches, skinned, stones removed and reserved, and sliced
1 kg raspberries, hulled and picked over

Imperial
2 lb sugar
½ pint dry white wine or water
grated rind and juice of 1 lemon
2 lb peaches, skinned, stones removed and reserved, and sliced
2 lb raspberries, hulled and picked over

Cooking time: about 30 minutes

Place the sugar, wine or water, lemon rind and juice in a large pan. Heat gently, stirring until the sugar is dissolved, then bring to the boil. Boil for 10 minutes until a syrup forms.
Crack open the peach stones with a hammer, skin the kernels and add them with the peaches and raspberries to the pan. Cook gently for 10 minutes or until tender but the fruit still retains its shape. Cool completely before pouring into prepared jars. Cover as for jam (see page 10).
Makes about 1¾ kg/4 lb

Brandied apricot and hazelnut conserve

Metric
1 kg dried apricots
2¼ litres water
500 g lemons
1¾ kg sugar
100 g hazelnuts,
    skinned
6 × 15 ml spoons brandy

Imperial
2 lb dried apricots
4 pints water
1 lb lemons
4 lb sugar
4 oz hazelnuts,
    skinned
6 tablespoons brandy

Cooking time: about 1 hour

Soak the apricots in the water overnight, or pour over boiling water and leave to soak for at least 2 hours.

Strain the apricots, reserving the soaking water. Pour the water into a large pan and add the grated rind of the lemons with the sugar. Heat gently, stirring until the sugar is dissolved, then bring to the boil. Boil for 15 minutes or until syrupy.

Cut off the pith from the lemons with a sharp knife and slice the flesh thinly. Add to the pan, together with the apricots, and boil for about 45 minutes or until the apricots are tender but still retain their shape, and the syrup is thick. Stir in the hazelnuts and brandy. Cool completely before pouring into prepared jars. Cover as for jam (see page 10).

Makes about 3 kg/7 lb

Spiced orange and walnut conserve

Metric
1¾ kg oranges
cold water to cover
1 litre water
1 kg sugar
1 kg honey
grated rind and juice of
    2 lemons
25 g root ginger,
    peeled and chopped
1 cinnamon stick
1 × 5 ml spoon cloves
100 g walnuts
100 g mixed cut peel

Imperial
4 lb oranges
cold water to cover
1¾ pints water
2 lb sugar
2 lb honey
grated rind and juice of
    2 lemons
1 oz root ginger,
    peeled and chopped
1 cinnamon stick
1 teaspoon cloves
4 oz walnuts
4 oz mixed cut peel

Cooking time: about 1¼ hours

Wipe the oranges and thinly peel off the rind with a potato peeler. Cut the rind into thin strips and place in a saucepan, cover with cold water, bring to the boil and simmer for 10 minutes, drain.

Cut all the pith away from the oranges, with a sharp knife, and reserve with the pips, then cut the flesh into slices, reserving all the juice. Add the orange juice to the pan with the water, sugar, honey and lemon rind and juice. Heat gently, stirring until the sugar and honey are dissolved.

Tie the orange and lemon pith and pips in a muslin bag with the ginger, cinnamon and cloves. Add the muslin bag to the syrup in the pan and bring to the boil. Reduce the heat and simmer for 45 to 60 minutes or until the orange rind strips are tender and the liquid is thick and syrupy and just beginning to turn a caramel colour.

Add the orange segments, walnuts and mixed cut peel to the pan and simmer gently for 5 minutes or until the orange segments are tender, and still retain their shape. Remove the muslin bag, squeezing well. Cool completely before pouring into prepared jars. Cover as for jam (see page 10).

Makes about 2¾ kg/6 lb

Left: Brandied apricot and hazelnut conserve

Spiced orange and walnut conserve; Spiced apple and rum conserve; Spiced cherry conserve

Spiced apple and rum conserve

Metric	Imperial
1 kg cooking apples, roughly cut up	2 lb cooking apples, roughly cut up
1.2 litres water	2 pints water
25 g root ginger, peeled and chopped	1 oz root ginger, peeled and chopped
grated rind and juice of 2 lemons	grated rind and juice of 2 lemons
approx 1¼ kg sugar	approx 2¾ lb sugar
225 g sultanas	8 oz sultanas
1 kg dessert apples	2 lb dessert apples
6 × 15 ml spoons rum (optional)	6 tablespoons rum (optional)

Cooking time: about 1½ hours

Place the cooking apples in a pan with the water, ginger and lemon rind. Cover the pan and bring to the boil. Reduce the heat and simmer for about 1 hour or until the apples are very soft. Rub the apple mixture through a sieve with a wooden spoon. Add the lemon juice to the apple purée, then measure and add 500 g/1 lb sugar for every 600 ml/1 pint purée.

Transfer the purée and sugar to a large pan and add the sultanas. Heat gently, stirring until the sugar is dissolved, then bring to the boil. Reduce the heat and simmer for 5 minutes.

Cut the dessert apples into quarters, core (peel if liked) and cut into thin slices. Add the apple slices to the pan and cook gently for 15 minutes or until the apple slices are tender but still retain their shape.

Stir in the rum, if used and cool completely before pouring into prepared jars. Cover as for jam (see page 10).

Makes about 3 kg/7 lb

Spiced cherry conserve

Metric	Imperial
1¾ kg red cherries, stoned	4 lb red cherries, stoned
1¾ kg sugar	4 lb sugar
grated rind and juice of 4 lemons (reserve pith and pips)	grated rind and juice of 4 lemons (reserve pith and pips)
1 cinnamon stick	1 cinnamon stick
1 × 5 ml spoon cloves	1 teaspoon cloves

Cooking time: about 1 hour

Layer the stoned cherries in a bowl with the sugar. Cover and leave overnight to firm the cherries and extract the juice.

Transfer the cherries, sugar and juice to a large pan. Add the lemon rind and juice. Place the reserved lemon pith and pips in a muslin bag, together with the cinnamon and cloves, and add to the pan. Heat gently, stirring until the sugar is dissolved, then bring to the boil. Reduce the heat and simmer for about 45 minutes or until the cherries are tender but retain their shape and the syrup is thick. Remove the muslin bag, squeezing well. Cool completely before pouring into prepared jars. Cover as for jam (see page 10).

Makes about 2½ kg/5½ lb

Rhubarb, orange and almond conserve

Metric	Imperial
1¾ kg rhubarb, cut into 1 cm slices	4 lb rhubarb, cut into ½ inch slices
1¾ kg sugar	4 lb sugar
4 oranges	4 oranges
100 g split almonds	4 oz split almonds
25 g root ginger, peeled and chopped	1 oz root ginger, peeled and chopped

Cooking time: about 30 minutes

Place the rhubarb in a bowl and layer with the sugar. Cover and leave for 24 hours, stirring occasionally, to extract the juice. Drain off the rhubarb and reserve. Transfer the juice and sugar to a large pan. Grate the rind from the oranges into the pan. Cut off the pith with a sharp knife and reserve with the pips; cut the flesh into segments between the membrane – do this over the pan to catch the juice.

Tie the orange pith and pips with the ginger in a muslin bag and add to the pan. Heat gently, stirring until the sugar is dissolved, then bring to the boil. Reduce the heat and simmer gently for about 15 minutes or until the fruit is tender but still retains its shape. Add the rhubarb and orange segments and simmer gently for about 15 minutes. Remove the muslin bag, squeezing well. Cool completely before spooning into prepared jars.
Cover as for jam (see page 10).
Makes about 3 kg/7 lb

Plum, orange and raisin conserve

Metric	Imperial
500 g oranges	1 lb oranges
1½ kg plums, stones removed and reserved	3 lb plums, stones removed and reserved
225 g stoned raisins	8 oz stoned raisins
1¾ kg honey	4 lb honey

Cooking time: about 30 minutes

Grate the rind from the oranges. Cut off all the white pith with a sharp knife and cut the flesh into slices; tie the orange pith and pips with the reserved plum stones in a muslin bag.

Place the honey, muslin bag and orange rind in a large saucepan. Heat gently to melt the honey, then bring to the boil and simmer for 10 minutes until syrupy. Add the plums, orange slices and raisins and simmer for about 15 minutes (or longer depending on the type of plum) or until the plums are tender and still retain their shape, and the honey syrup is thick. Remove the muslin bag, squeezing well. Cool completely before pouring into prepared jars. Cover as for jam (see page 10).
Makes about 3 kg/7 lb

Rhubarb, orange and almond conserve; Grapefruit conserve; Plum, orange and raisin conserve

Grapefruit conserve

Metric	Imperial
2¾ kg grapefruit	6 lb grapefruit
(about 8 medium)	(about 8 medium)
1¾ kg sugar	4 lb sugar
500 g glacé cherries	1 lb glacé cherries

Cooking time: about 1 hour

Wipe the grapefruit and grate the rind into a saucepan. Cut off all the white pith with a sharp knife and reserve with the pips. Cut the flesh into segments between the membranes, reserving the juice. Add all the juice and the sugar to the saucepan. Heat gently, stirring until the sugar is dissolved.

Tie the pith and pips in a muslin bag and add to the pan. Simmer for 30 minutes or until the mixture is syrupy and thick. Remove the muslin bag, squeezing it well.

Add the grapefruit segments and cherries and bring to the boil. Reduce the heat and simmer gently for about 10 minutes when the fruit should be suspended in a thick syrup but still retain its shape. Cool completely before pouring into prepared jars. Cover as for jam (see page 10).

Makes about 1¾ kg/4 lb

CURDS, CHEESES, BUTTERS AND MINCEMEAT

Curds, cheeses and butters are rich preserves using a high proportion of fruit and giving a comparatively small yield. They can be made with fruit jellies using the pulp, the juice being strained for the jelly.

CURDS

This is a rich fruit custard of fruit purée cooked lightly with butter and eggs. Its storage life is short because of the ingredients – about 1 month in a cupboard or up to 3 months in a refrigerator. Ideal for spreading on bread, curds also make delicious fillings for tarts and cakes.

The fruit juice or purée is cooked with sugar, butter and eggs until it thickens: it is then poured into prepared jars (see jam-making, page 10) where it will thicken more on cooling. The mixture must not boil as the eggs may curdle, therefore it is usually cooked in a double saucepan.

CHEESES

This delightful old-fashioned preserve used to be served instead of the cheese course, hence its name. Now it is cut in slices and served with meats and bread.

The fruit pulp is sieved, and then cooked with an equal quantity of sugar to a thick purée. The cheese is ready when a wooden spoon drawn through the mixture shows the bottom of the pan in a clean line before the mixture slowly falls back; and large flat bubbles appear on the surface. Spoon the mixture immediately into oiled wide-necked jars or jelly moulds and cover as for jam (see page 10); large moulds can be covered with a layer of melted paraffin wax to seal. Due to their high sugar quantity, fruit cheeses keep well for about 2 years and improve with keeping for several months.

BUTTERS

This is similar to a cheese but with a softer, spreading consistency like a curd. They do not keep well – 3 to 6 months – so cover (see page 10) and store them carefully.

MINCEMEAT

This is a delicious spiced mixture of fresh and dried fruit, preserved with sugar and alcohol.

Lemon curd

Metric	Imperial
4 medium lemons	4 medium lemons
100 g butter	4 oz butter
350 g granulated or caster sugar	12 oz granulated or caster sugar
4 eggs, lightly beaten	4 eggs, lightly beaten

Cooking time: about 30 minutes

Grate the lemon rind into a basin, then add the squeezed juice. Cut the butter into pieces, and add it with the sugar. Strain the eggs into the basin. Place the basin over a pan of simmering water, then stir until the sugar has dissolved and the butter melted. Continue to cook, stirring constantly, until the curd thickens enough to coat the back of a wooden spoon. Do not overcook, as the eggs may curdle. Pour into prepared jars and cover with a waxed disc and cellophane as for jam.
Keeps for 1 month, or 3 months refrigerated.
Makes about 750 g/1¾ lb

Variations:
Substitute 3 oranges and 1 lemon for the lemons.

Concentrated orange curd; Lemon curd; Spiced apple curd

Concentrated orange curd

Metric	Imperial
175 ml can frozen unsweetened concentrated orange juice, thawed	6 fl oz can frozen unsweetened concentrated orange juice, thawed
100 g butter	4 oz butter
350 g sugar	12 oz sugar
4 eggs, lightly beaten	4 eggs, lightly beaten

Cooking time: about 30 minutes

Pour the thawed concentrated juice into a basin. Cut the butter into pieces, and add it with the sugar. Strain the eggs into the basin. Place the basin over a pan of simmering water, then stir until the sugar has dissolved and the butter melted.

Continue to cook, stirring constantly, until the curd thickens enough to coat the back of a wooden spoon. Pour into prepared jars and cover with a waxed disc and cellophane as for jam.

Keeps for 1 month, or 3 months refrigerated.

Makes about 750 g/1¾ lb

Variation:
Substitute concentrated grapefruit juice for the orange juice.

Spiced apple curd

Metric	Imperial
500 g cooking apples, peeled, cored and chopped	1 lb cooking apples, peeled, cored and chopped
grated rind and juice of 1 lemon	grated rind and juice of 1 lemon
100 g butter	4 oz butter
350 g sugar	12 oz sugar
1 × 5 ml spoon ground ginger	1 teaspoon ground ginger
1 × 5 ml spoon ground cinnamon	1 teaspoon ground cinnamon
4 eggs, lightly beaten	4 eggs, lightly beaten

Cooking time: about 40 minutes

Place the apples in a saucepan with the lemon rind and juice. Cover and cook gently, stirring occasionally, for about 15 minutes or until the apples are soft and pulpy. Remove from the heat and beat well until smooth, or for a smoother purée, rub through a sieve. Cut the butter into pieces, and add it with the sugar and spices. Strain in the eggs. Transfer the mixture to a basin placed over a pan of simmering water, and stir until the sugar has dissolved and the butter melted.

Continue to cook, stirring constantly, until the curd thickens enough to coat the back of a wooden spoon. Pour into prepared jars and cover with a waxed disc and cellophane as for jam.

Keeps for 1 month, or 3 months refrigerated.

Makes about 1 kg/2¼ lb

Strawberry curd

Metric	Imperial
225 g strawberries	*8 oz strawberries*
grated rind and juice	*grated rind and juice*
of 1 orange	*of 1 orange*
100 g butter	*4 oz butter*
350 g sugar	*12 oz sugar*
4 eggs, lightly beaten	*4 eggs, lightly beaten*

Cooking time: about 30 minutes

Place the strawberries in a basin and mash lightly with
a fork. Add the orange rind and juice. Cut the butter
into pieces, and add it with the sugar. Strain the
eggs into the basin.
Place the basin over a pan of simmering water, then
stir until the sugar has dissolved and the butter
melted. Continue to cook, stirring constantly, until the
curd thickens enough to coat the back of a wooden
spoon. Pour into prepared jars and cover with a waxed
disc and cellophane as for jam.
Keeps for 1 month, or 3 months refrigerated.
Makes about 1 kg/2¼ lb

Variation:
Substitute a lemon for the orange.

Raspberry curd

Metric	Imperial
350 g raspberries	*12 oz raspberries*
225 g cooking apples,	*8 oz cooking apples,*
peeled, cored and	*peeled, cored and*
chopped	*chopped*
grated rind and juice of	*grated rind and juice of*
1 lemon	*1 lemon*
100 g butter	*4 oz butter*
350 g sugar	*12 oz sugar*
4 eggs, lightly beaten	*4 eggs, lightly beaten*

Cooking time: about 45 minutes

Place the raspberries, apple, lemon rind and juice in a
saucepan. Cover and bring to the boil, stirring
occasionally. Reduce the heat, then simmer for 15
minutes or until the fruit is soft. Purée the mixture
by rubbing through a sieve into a basin. Cut the
butter into pieces, and add it with the sugar. Strain
in the eggs.
Place the basin over a pan of simmering water, then
stir until the sugar has dissolved and the butter
melted. Continue to cook, stirring constantly, until
the curd thickens enough to coat the back of a wooden
spoon. Pour into prepared jars and cover with a waxed
disc and cellophane as for jam.
Keeps for 1 month, or 3 months refrigerated.
Makes about 1 kg/2¼ lb

Strawberry curd; Raspberry curd; Tomato curd

Tomato curd

Metric	Imperial
500 g tomatoes, roughly chopped	1 lb tomatoes, roughly chopped
grated rind and juice of 1 lemon	grated rind and juice of 1 lemon
sprig of mint	sprig of mint
100 g butter	4 oz butter
350 g sugar	12 oz sugar
4 eggs, lightly beaten	4 eggs, lightly beaten

Cooking time: about 40 minutes

Place the tomatoes, lemon rind and juice and mint in a saucepan. Cover and cook gently for 10 minutes or until the tomatoes are pulpy. Purée the mixture by rubbing through a sieve into a basin. Cut the butter into pieces, and add it with the sugar. Strain in the beaten eggs.

Place the basin over a pan of simmering water, then stir until the sugar has dissolved and the butter melted. Continue to cook, stirring constantly, until the curd thickens enough to coat the back of a wooden spoon. Pour into prepared jars and cover with a waxed disc and cellophane as for jam.

Keeps for 1 month, or 3 months refrigerated.

Makes about 750 g/1¾ lb

Apricot and orange cheese

Apricot and orange cheese

Metric	Imperial
1 kg dried apricots	2 lb dried apricots
2 litres water	3½ pints water
approx 1¾ kg sugar	approx 4 lb sugar
grated rind and juice of 4 oranges	grated rind and juice of 4 oranges

Cooking time: about 2 hours

Soak the apricots in the water overnight, or pour on boiling water and soak for 2 hours. Transfer to a saucepan, with the water, cover and cook for about 1 hour or until soft. Liquidize the apricots with the water, or rub through a sieve.

Weigh the apricot purée and add 500 g/1 lb sugar for every 500 g/1 lb purée. Return the purée to a clean saucepan with the sugar and orange rind and juice. Stir over a gentle heat until the sugar has dissolved. Continue to cook, stirring, until the purée is very thick. A spoon drawn across the bottom of the pan should leave a firm clean line through the mixture. Pour at once into prepared oiled jars or moulds. Cover with a waxed disc and cellophane as for jam.

Keeps for up to 2 years.

Makes about 2 kg/4½ lb

Spiced cranberry and apple cheese

Bramble butter

Metric	Imperial
1 kg blackberries	2 lb blackberries
1 kg cooking apples, roughly chopped	2 lb cooking apples, roughly chopped
grated rind and juice of 2 lemons	grated rind and juice of 2 lemons
approx 1 kg sugar	approx 2 lb sugar

Cooking time: about 45 minutes

There is no need to peel the apples for this recipe.

Place the blackberries in a saucepan with the apples and lemon rind and juice. Cover and cook gently for 15 minutes or until the fruit is soft and pulpy. Rub through a sieve and weigh the purée.
Return the purée to the pan and add 350 g/12 oz sugar for each 500 g/1 lb purée. Bring slowly to the boil, stirring until the sugar has dissolved. Continue to cook to a thick creamy consistency. Pour into prepared oiled jars or moulds, and cover with a waxed disc and cellophane as for jam.
Keeps for 3 to 6 months.
Makes about 1½ kg/3 lb

Variation:
Substitute oranges for the lemons.

Spiced cranberry and apple cheese

Metric	Imperial
1 kg cranberries	2 lb cranberries
1 kg cooking apples, chopped	2 lb cooking apples, chopped
grated rind and juice of 4 oranges	grated rind and juice of 4 oranges
1 × 5 ml spoon cloves	1 teaspoon cloves
1 cinnamon stick	1 cinnamon stick
2 mace blades	2 mace blades
600 ml water	1 pint water
approx 1¾ kg sugar	approx 4 lb sugar

Cooking time: about 1½ hours

Place the cranberries, apples, orange rind and juice and the spices in a saucepan. Pour over the water and cover the pan. Bring to the boil, then simmer for about 30 minutes or until the fruit is soft and pulpy. Rub through a sieve and weigh the purée.
Return it to the pan and add 500 g/1 lb sugar for every 500 g/1 lb purée. Stir over a low heat until the sugar dissolves. Continue to cook, stirring until the purée is very thick. A spoon drawn across the bottom of the pan should leave a clean firm line through the mixture. Pour at once into prepared oiled jars or moulds. Cover with a waxed disc and cellophane as for jam.
Keeps for up to 2 years.
Makes about 1¾ kg/4 lb

Cidered apple butter

Metric	Imperial
1¾ kg cooking apples, chopped	4 lb cooking apples, chopped
1.2 litres cider	2 pints cider
1 cinnamon stick	1 cinnamon stick
1 × 5 ml spoon cloves	1 teaspoon cloves
approx 1½ kg granulated or brown sugar	approx 3 lb granulated or brown sugar

Place the apples in a saucepan with the cider, cinnamon and cloves. Cover and cook gently, stirring occasionally, for about 20 minutes or until soft and pulpy. Rub through a sieve and weigh the purée.
Add 350 g/12 oz sugar for every 500 g/1 lb purée.
Return the purée with the sugar to a clean saucepan. Stir over a gentle heat until the sugar dissolves. Continue to cook for about 20 minutes, stirring occasionally, until it is a thick creamy consistency. Pour into prepared oiled jars, and cover with a waxed disc and cellophane as for jam.
Keeps for 3 to 6 months.
Makes about 2¼ kg/5 lb

Right, top shelf: Bramble butter; Cidered apple butter; Rhubarb butter. Bottom shelf: Mincemeat

Rhubarb butter

Metric	Imperial
1½ kg rhubarb, chopped	3 lb rhubarb, chopped
grated rind and juice of 4 oranges	grated rind and juice of 4 oranges
approx 750 g granulated sugar	approx 1½ lb granulated sugar

Cooking time: about 30 minutes

Place the rhubarb in a saucepan with the orange rind and juice. Cover the pan and stew gently for 15 minutes or until the rhubarb is soft, stirring. Remove from the heat and beat well to a pulp. Weigh the pulp. Add 225 g/8 oz sugar for every 500 g/1 lb pulp. Stir over a gentle heat until the sugar dissolves. Continue to cook for about 15 minutes, stirring occasionally, until it reaches a thick creamy consistency. Pour into prepared oiled jars, and cover with a waxed disc and cellophane as for jam.
Keeps for 3 to 6 months.
Makes about 1¾ kg/4 lb

Mincemeat

Metric	Imperial
1 kg cooking apples, peeled, cored and coarsely grated or minced	2 lb cooking apples, peeled, cored and coarsely grated or minced
500 g sultanas	1 lb sultanas
500 g currants	1 lb currants
500 g raisins, stoned	1 lb raisins, stoned
500 g shredded suet	1 lb shredded suet
500 g demerara sugar	1 lb demerara sugar
225 g mixed cut peel	8 oz mixed cut peel
225 g almonds, chopped or flaked	8 oz almonds, chopped or flaked
grated rind and juice of 2 lemons	grated rind and juice of 2 lemons
150 ml brandy	¼ pint brandy
1 × 5 ml spoon mixed spice	1 teaspoon mixed spice
1 × 5 ml spoon ground ginger	1 teaspoon ground ginger
1 × 5 ml spoon ground cinnamon	1 teaspoon ground cinnamon
1 × 2.5 ml spoon grated nutmeg	½ teaspoon grated nutmeg

Store mincemeat for at least three months before using, to allow the flavours to mature.

Place all the ingredients in a bowl and combine well. Cover, then leave for 1 to 2 days to allow the flavours to blend. Mix well again before spooning into the prepared jars. Cover with a waxed disc and cellophane as for jam.
Keeps for at least 1 year.
Makes about 3½ kg/8 lb

Variations:
Substitute pears for the apples.
Substitute sherry or cider for the brandy.
Substitute other dried fruits, e.g. apricots or figs for the sultanas, currants and raisins, or use glacé fruits instead of mixed cut peel.
Add 225 g/8 oz grapes, quartered and deseeded per 1 kg/2 lb mincemeat. This mincemeat will only keep for about 2 weeks.

BOTTLING

Bottling is a very traditional and easy way of preserving fruits by heat treatment. The fruit is heated in special vacuum bottles or jam jars to sterilize it by killing all spoilage micro-organisms present in the fruit; then an airtight seal is made while the fruit is hot to prevent other spoilage micro-organisms from entering and thus causing the fruit to ferment or go bad. It is important that the bottling process is carried out correctly if the fruit is to be preserved, but once the rules have been mastered bottling becomes a very simple and rewarding process.

Home bottling of vegetables is not recommended as they lack sufficient acidity to prevent spoilage and temperatures are not high enough to guarantee complete sterilization.

TYPES OF VACUUM BOTTLES

There are two types of vacuum bottles for bottling, both are available in different sizes ranging from 500 g/1 lb to 1¾ kg/4 lb.

Clip bottles: these have metal or glass lids separated from the bottle by a rubber ring. The lid is secured by a metal spring clip, which allows air and steam to escape during processing and keeps the lid in position during cooling to form a vacuum.

Screw-band bottles: these have metal or glass lids separated from the bottle by a rubber ring. The lid is secured by a metal or plastic screw-band which is screwed on lightly during processing and tightened during cooling to form a vacuum.

Jam jars: these can be used for bottling if special metal or glass covers with rubber or plastic rings and clips at the side are used for sealing. They can also be covered with a special preserving skin, which should be used according to the manufacturer's instructions (the skin will shrink into the jar after processing to form a vacuum).

All bottles, jars and lids must be free from chips and cracks, and rubber rings and metal lids must only be used once to ensure a perfect seal. The bottles must be washed thoroughly, rinsed and left to drain – they are easier to fill if they are still wet inside. If bottles are very dirty, sterilize them by immersing in a pan of cold water, bringing to the boil and boiling for 5 minutes. Rubber rings should be soaked in warm water for 15 minutes, then dipped in boiling water immediately before using.

FILLING THE BOTTLES

Fruit must be in good condition, so discard any over-ripe or spoiled fruit. Wash and prepare fruits according to type, e.g. hull soft fruits; top and tail gooseberries and currants; remove pith and peel from citrus fruits and cut into segments or slices. Apples and pears should be peeled, cored and cut into quarters or slices; stone fruit such as plums, peaches, etc, can be bottled whole or halved and stoned.

Pack the fruit tightly into the prepared wet bottles or jars, pressing down gently with the handle of a wooden spoon and taking care not to bruise the fruit. Fill the bottle or jar to within 1 to 2.5 cm/½ to 1 inch from the top.

The choice of liquid is water or syrup; the best colour and flavour is produced when syrup is used but it causes the fruit to rise in the bottles. The average proportions of sugar to water for a syrup are 225 g/8 oz sugar to 600 ml/1 pint water; honey or golden syrup may be substituted for sugar.

A syrup can also be flavoured with whole spices, lemon or orange rind and then strained before filling into bottles or jars, or with liqueurs, spirits or wine.

To prepare the syrup, slowly heat the sugar with the water, stirring until it is dissolved, then add flavourings if used and boil for 1 minute. Pour the syrup or water, hot or cold depending on the method used (see below), over the fruit in the bottles, tilting them to exclude any air bubbles. Be sure to stand hot bottles or jars on a wooden surface or other non-conductor of heat or they may crack. Then dip rubber bands in boiling water, fit them on the bottles, then put on the lids, followed immediately by the clip or screwband. In the case of the latter, loosen them by about a quarter turn to allow steam and air to escape during processing or they may burst.

METHODS OF PROCESSING BOTTLES

There are several methods of bottling fruit, depending on the equipment and time available. The two oven methods use more fuel than any of the three top of the stove methods, and temperatures cannot be controlled so easily.

Moderate oven method: this is probably the easiest processing method and requires no special equipment. More bottles or jars can be processed at any one time, although it takes longer than when done on top of the stove.

Warm the jars in a preheated cool oven (150°C/300°F, Gas Mark 2). Fill them with fruit and then pour over boiling water or syrup to within 2.5 cm/1 inch of the top. Place the rubber rings and lids on the jars but without the clips or screws. Place the bottles 5 cm/2 inches apart on a baking sheet (line with newspaper, cardboard or an asbestos mat or even a little water so that any syrup boiling out won't burn in the oven). Cook for 30 minutes to 1½ hours depending on the fruit (see chart on page 57) and the number and size of jars in the oven at any one time. Remove the jars from the oven and secure the lids with clips or screw-bands immediately and leave to cool on a wooden surface.

PREPARATION CHART

CATEGORY	FRUIT	PREPARATION	WASTE FROM 500 g/1 lb OF FRUIT		PREPARED FRUIT PER 500 g/1 lb or 500 ml/18 fl oz JAR	
A	Apples	Peel, core, slice, ring or quarter	100–175 g	4–6 oz	275 g	10 oz
	Gooseberries	Top and tail, nicking skin to prevent shrivelling	25 g	1 oz	275–350 g	10–12 oz
	Rhubarb	Remove leaves and base, wash and cut into even lengths 2.5–5 cm/1–2 inch	50–100 g	2–4 oz	275 g	10 oz
	Blackberries	Remove stalks, maggots and damaged fruit	25–50 g	1–2 oz	275–350 g	10–12 oz
	Blueberries/ Bilberries	Remove stalks	25–50 g	1–2 oz	350 g	12 oz
	Currants	Remove stems	25–75 g	1–3 oz	350 g	12 oz
	Raspberries/ Loganberries	Remove stalks and plugs, maggots and damaged fruit	25–50 g	1–2 oz	350–400 g	12–14 oz
	Strawberries	Remove stalks	25 g	1 oz	250 g	9 oz
B	Citrus fruit	Cut off peel and pith, cut into rings/ segments, remove pips	200–350 g	7–12 oz	350–425 g	12–15 oz
	Apricots	Remove stalks, rinse	25–50 g	1–2 oz	275 g	10 oz
	Cherries	Remove stalks, rinse, remove stones if liked	25–75 g	1–3 oz	350 g	12 oz
			50–150 g	2–5 oz	350 g	12 oz
	Peaches	Peel by blanching ¼–1 minute	50–100 g	2–4 oz	250–350 g	9–12 oz
	Plums	Remove stalks, rinse	25–50 g	1–2 oz	275–350 g	10–12 oz
C	Halved stone fruit	Prepare as above, halve and stone	50–225 g	2–8 oz	350–425 g	12–15 oz
	Pineapple	Remove peel and core, cut into rings or chunks	Varies		350 g	12 oz
	Tight-pack apples	Peel, core, slice, blanch 2 minutes to soften	100–175 g	4–6 oz	425 g	15 oz
	Tight-pack strawberries	Cover with boiling syrup and soak overnight, drain and pack. Concentrate syrup	25 g	1 oz	500 g	1 lb
D	Figs	Remove stems	25–100 g	1–4 oz	225 g	8 oz
	Pears	Peel, halve and core	100–175 g	4–6 oz	225–350 g	8–12 oz
	Quinces/ Cooking pears	Peel, halve and core. Stew in syrup first	100–175 g	4–6 oz	225–350 g	8–12 oz

Slow oven method: this is most suitable for dark-coloured fruits as light-coloured fruits may brown.

Pack the fruit into the prepared jars, but do not pour over syrup or liquid. Place the lids on top but do not add rubber rings, clips or screw-bands. Place the bottles on a baking sheet as for the moderate oven method in a preheated very cool oven (120°C/250°F, Gas Mark ½). Cook for 45 minutes to 1½ hours, depending on the type of fruit (see chart opposite) and quantity of bottles in the oven. Remove the jars, one at a time, from the oven and immediately fill to the brim with boiling syrup or water (the bottles may also be topped up with cooked fruit from another jar if the fruit has shrunk in the bottle). Dip rubber bands in boiling water and fit on the bottles, replace the hot lids and secure with clips or screw-bands immediately. Leave to cool on a board.

Slow water bath method: this probably gives fruit the best appearance.

Pack the fruit into the prepared jars, and pour in cold syrup or water. Place the lids on top, with their rubber bands, and secure with clips or screw-bands, loosened by a quarter turn.

Place a trivet, a thick cloth, or wad of newspaper in the base of a deep saucepan so that the jars do not come into direct contact with the base of the pan. Place the filled jars in the pan, taking care they do not touch each other or the sides of the pan. Completely cover the bottles with cold water; if the bottles cannot be submerged, the water must come at least to the shoulder of the bottles, and the pan covered with a tight-fitting lid.

Heat the water gently from cold to 55°C/130°F in 1 hour, and the required temperature (74 to 88°C/165 to 190°F according to the type of fruit – see chart below) in another 30 minutes. When the required heating time is up, remove the bottles with tongs. Place on a wooden board; tighten screw-bands, if used.

Quick water bath method: this is similar to the slow water bath method but no thermometer is necessary and the bottles are filled with hot syrup and placed in warm water.

Pack prepared bottles with fruit and fill with hot syrup (60°C/140°F). Cover the bottles as for the slow water bath method and immerse in hand-hot water (38°C/100°F). Bring the water to simmering point (88°C/190°F) in 30 minutes, then simmer for the appropriate processing time (see the chart below). Remove the bottles and finish as for the slow water bath method.

Pressure cooker method: use the cooker according to the manufacturer's instructions but in general the procedure is as follows:

Pack the fruit into the prepared bottles and fill with boiling syrup or water. Cover the bottles as for the slow water bath method.

Preheat 2.5 cm/1 inch water (about 900 ml/1½ pints) in the pressure cooker with a trivet fitted in the base. Place bottles in the pan so they do not touch each other or the sides of the pan. Cover the pan and bring to Low/5 lb pressure over moderate heat (this should take between 5 to 10 minutes). Maintain pressure for the time required, from 1 to 5 minutes depending on the type of fruit (see chart on page 57). Remove pan from the heat and leave to cool for 10 minutes before opening.

The total processing time is 5 to 10 minutes coming to pressure, plus 1 to 5 minutes held at pressure, plus 10 minutes cooling, which should be timed carefully as during this time the bottles are still being processed. Remove the bottles and seal as for slow water bath method.

TESTING THE SEAL

When the bottles are completely cold after processing, preferably the next day, test to make sure a vacuum has formed. Remove clips or screw-bands and carefully lift up each bottle by

BOTTLING CHART

CATEGORY (see chart opposite)	QUANTITY	MODERATE OVEN	SLOW OVEN	SLOW WATER BATH	QUICK WATER BATH	PRESSURE COOKER
Follow carefully the instructions given for the different methods.		(see page 55)	(see opposite)	(see opposite)	(see above)	(see above)
A	Weight: 500 g–1¾ kg/1–4 lb Liquid: 500 ml–2 lit/18 fl oz–3½ pints	30–40 mins	45–55 mins	74°C/165°F 10 mins	2 mins	1 min
	Weight: 2¼–4½ kg/5–10 lb Liquid: 2½–5 lit/4½–9 pints	45–60 mins	60–75 mins	10 mins	2 mins	1 min
B	Weight: 500 g–1¾ kg/1–4 lb Liquid: 500 ml–2 lit/18 fl oz–3½ pints	40–50 mins	55–70 mins	82°C/180°F 15 mins	10 mins	1 min
	Weight: 2¼–4½ kg/5–10 lb Liquid: 2½–5 lit/4½–9 pints	55–70 mins	75–90 mins Not recommended for light fruits	15 mins	10 mins	1 min
C	Weight: 500 g–1¾ kg/1–4 lb Liquid: 500 ml–2 lit/18 fl oz–3½ pints	50–60 mins	Not recommended	82°C/180°F 15 mins	20 mins	3–4 mins
	Weight: 2¼–4½ kg/5–10 lb Liquid: 2½–5 lit/4½–9 pints	65–80 mins	Not recommended	15 mins	20 mins	3–4 mins
D	Weight: 500 g–1¾ kg/1–4 lb Liquid: 500 ml–2 lit/18 fl oz–3½ pints	60–70 mins	Not recommended	88°C/190°F 30 mins	40 mins	5 mins
	Weight: 2¼–4½ kg/5–10 lb Liquid: 2½–5 lit/4½–9 pints	75–90 mins	Not recommended	30 mins	40 mins	5 mins

Three types of jars suitable for bottling: clip bottles, screw-band bottles and jam jars with special covers

its lid. If the lid remains attached a vacuum has formed. If the lid falls off the fruit must be reprocessed or used as soon as possible and stored in the refrigerator meanwhile. Jars covered with preserving skin will be sealed correctly if the skin has been drawn down to form a hollow.

Wash and dry clips and screw-bands. Don't replace clips on the bottles as this can stretch them. However, screw-bands can be screwed on loosely, but they should be brushed lightly inside with oil to prevent rust.

STORING FILLED BOTTLES

After testing the seal on bottles, wipe them clean, particularly round the neck, label them and store in a cool, dark place. To open bottles, insert the point of a knife between the rubber seal and the bottle and prise off the lid – a stream of air bubbles will enter when the seal is broken. If the bottles are difficult to open, stand them in hot water for a few minutes.

Bottled red fruit compôte

Metric	Imperial
500 g red currants, stalks removed	1 lb red currants, stalks removed
500 g raspberries, stalks removed	1 lb raspberries, stalks removed
500 g red cherries, stoned	1 lb red cherries, stoned
450 ml water	¾ pint water
350 g sugar	12 oz sugar

Cooking time: about 45 minutes

Mix the fruits together. Make the syrup by gently heating the water with the sugar and stirring until dissolved, then bring to the boil and boil for 1 minute. Pack the fruits into the prepared bottles and pour over the boiling syrup. Place the rubber rings and lids on the bottles, but without clips or screw-bands.

Stand the bottles on a baking sheet lined with newspaper, 5 cm/2 inches apart. Place in the centre of a preheated cool oven (150°C/300°F, Gas Mark 2) and cook for 30 minutes.

Remove the bottles from the oven and secure immediately with clips or screw-bands and leave to cool. When completely cold test the seal, then wipe clean, label and store.

Makes about 1¾ kg/4 lb

Bottled fruit salad

Metric	Imperial
450 ml water	¾ pint water
350 g sugar	12 oz sugar
grated rind and juice of 2 lemons	grated rind and juice of 2 lemons
500 g apples, quartered, cored and sliced (peel if liked)	1 lb apples, quartered, cored and sliced (peel if liked)
500 g pears, peeled, quartered, cored and sliced	1 lb pears, peeled, quartered, cored and sliced
500 g oranges, peel and pith removed, cut into slices	1 lb oranges, peel and pith removed, cut into slices
500 g peaches, peeled, halved, stoned and sliced	1 lb peaches, peeled, halved, stoned and sliced
225 g green grapes, halved and seeded	8 oz green grapes, halved and seeded

Cooking time: about 1 hour

Other fruits, than those above, may be substituted, but remember that dark fruits will colour the fruit salad.
Other bottling methods may be used for this fruit salad.

Prepare the syrup first so that the prepared fruit will not go brown. Place the water, sugar and lemon rind in a saucepan. Heat gently, stirring to dissolve the sugar, then bring to the boil and boil for 1 minute.
Toss the fruit lightly in some of the lemon juice to prevent browning. Carefully pack the fruit into the prepared warm jars. Add the reserved lemon juice to the syrup and return to the boil. Pour the boiling syrup over the fruit. Place the rubber rings and lids on the bottles but without clips or screw-bands.
Stand the bottles on a baking sheet lined with newspaper, 5 cm/2 inches apart. Place in the centre of a pre-heated cool oven (150°C/300°F, Gas Mark 2) and cook for 45 minutes.
Remove the bottles from the oven and secure immediately with clips or screw-bands and leave to cool. When completely cold test the seal, then wipe clean, label and store.
Makes about 1¾ kg/4 lb

Bottled red fruit compôte; Bottled fruit salad

From left: Pears in red wine;
Dry-pack bottled strawberries (finished and in preparation);
Solid-pack tomatoes; Tomatoes in brine

Pears in red wine

Metric	*Imperial*
600 ml red wine	*1 pint red wine*
600 ml water	*1 pint water*
225 g sugar	*8 oz sugar*
4 × 15 ml spoons red currant jelly	*4 tablespoons red currant jelly*
4 strips lemon rind	*4 strips lemon rind*
1 cinnamon stick	*1 cinnamon stick*
2 kg cooking pears	*4½ lb cooking pears*

Cooking time: about 1½ hours

For this recipe, any of the other bottling methods may also be used.

Pour the wine and water into a saucepan and add the sugar, red currant jelly, lemon rind and cinnamon. Heat gently, stirring until the sugar and jelly dissolve. Bring to the boil and boil for 2 minutes.
Cut the pears in half lengthways, remove the cores and stalks and peel. Place the pear halves in the simmering wine syrup and cook gently for about 15 minutes or until the pears are just tender, but keep their shape. Remove the pears with a slotted spoon and carefully pack into prepared bottles. Pour over the boiling wine syrup. Place rubber rings and lids on the bottles, but without clips or screw-bands.
Stand the bottles on a baking sheet lined with newspaper, 5 cm/2 inches apart, to allow the hot air to circulate. Place in the centre of a preheated cool oven (150°C/300°F, Gas Mark 2) and cook for 1 hour.
Remove the bottles from the oven and secure immediately with clips or screw-bands, then leave to cool. When completely cold test the seal, then wipe clean, label and store.
Makes about 1¾ kg/4 lb

Dry-pack bottled strawberries

Metric	*Imperial*
1½ kg strawberries, hulled	*3 lb strawberries, hulled*
350 g caster sugar	*12 oz caster sugar*

Cooking time: about 1 hour

Pack the prepared fruit into the bottles, layering with the sugar as you go. Put the lids on top but without the rubber rings and clips or screw-bands.
Stand the bottles on a baking sheet, lined with newspaper, 5 cm/2 inches apart. Place in the centre of a preheated cool oven (120°C/250°F, Gas Mark ½) and cook for 45 minutes.
Remove the bottles from the oven and, using the contents from one bottle, top up the remaining jars with fruit and juice. Put on the rubber rings, replace the lids and put on the clips or slightly loosened screw-bands. Return the bottles to the oven for a further 15 minutes until heated through.
Remove the bottles from the oven and tighten the screwbands, then leave to cool. When completely cold test the seal, then wipe clean, label and store.
Makes about 1½ kg/3 lb

Variation:
You can substitute raspberries, stalks removed, for the strawberries.

Solid-pack tomatoes

Metric	Imperial
1¾ kg tomatoes, skinned, halved or quartered	4 lb tomatoes, skinned, halved or quartered
4 × 15 ml spoons lemon juice or 2 × 5 ml spoons citric acid	4 tablespoons lemon juice or 2 teaspoons citric acid
2 × 15 ml spoons caster sugar	2 tablespoons caster sugar
1 × 15 ml spoon salt	1 tablespoon salt
sprigs of fresh herbs (mint, oregano, basil or thyme)	sprigs of fresh herbs (mint, oregano, basil or thyme)

Tomatoes in brine

Metric	Imperial
1¼ kg small tomatoes	2½ lb small tomatoes
5 × 15 ml spoons lemon juice or 2 × 5 ml spoons citric acid	5 tablespoons lemon juice or 2 teaspoons citric acid
1 × 15 ml spoon salt	1 tablespoon salt
1.2 litres water	2 pints water

Wash the tomatoes and pack tightly into the prepared jars. For the brine dissolve the lemon juice or citric acid and salt in the water and pour (hot or cold depending on the processing method used) over the tomatoes. Cover the jars and process according to the chosen method (see chart below).
Makes about 1¾ kg/4 lb

Pack prepared tomatoes carefully and as tightly as possible into the prepared bottles, layering them with the lemon juice, sugar, salt and herbs.
Cover the jars and process according to the chosen method (see chart below).
Makes about 1¾ kg/4 lb

PROCESSING TIMES FOR BOTTLED TOMATOES

BOTTLING METHOD	WEIGHT	MODERATE OVEN	SLOW WATER BATH (88°C/190°F)	QUICK WATER BATH	PRESSURE COOKER
Solid pack	500 g–1¾ kg/1–4 lb	70–80 mins	40 mins	50 mins	15 mins
	2¼–4½ kg/5–10 lb	85–100 mins	40 mins	50 mins	15 mins
Whole in brine	500 ml–2 lit/18 fl oz–3½ pints	60–70 mins	30 mins	40 mins	5 mins
	2½–5 lit/4½–9 pints	75–90 mins	30 mins	40 mins	5 mins

DRINKS

Home-made fruit drinks can easily be preserved by the fruit bottling process (see page 54).

SYRUPS AND JUICES

Syrups are made from strained fruit juice sweetened with sugar; they can be used in a concentrated form for flavouring and sauces or diluted with water, soda or milk for refreshing and economical drinks. Juices are unstrained fruit juice, often with grated rind added, mixed with sugar and water and served as a drink.

EXTRACTING THE JUICE

This can be done in several ways:
a) Heat – cooking with or without water, depending on the fruit.
b) Fermentation – yeasts in the fruit extract the juice if it is crushed and left in a warm place. The juice is strained off when bubbles appear on the surface.
c) Mechanical – with a liquidizer, juice extractor or squeezer.
d) Pectin-destroying enzyme – this extraction method is similar to fermentation, but a commercial product is added to the crushed fruit to break down the fruit tissue.

   Citric acid, available from chemists, may be added to give extra sharpness.

FILLING THE BOTTLES

Any bottles may be used as long as they withstand boiling, but small screw-top bottles are the most convenient to sterilize and use. Traditionally bottles are topped with corks and sealed with melted paraffin wax. Bottles and tops or corks should first be sterilized by placing in a pan, covering with water, bringing to the boil and boiling for several minutes. Fill screw-top bottles to within 2.5 cm/1 inch of the top and corked bottles to within 3.5 cm/1½ inches of the top to leave room for expansion on heating.

STERILIZING THE BOTTLES

This can be done by heat process, as in fruit bottling (see page 55) or by chemical process using Campden fruit preserving tablets.
Heat process: place the bottles on a trivet or false bottom in a deep saucepan as for bottling (loosely fit screw-tops and secure corks with string or fine wire). Fill the pan with cold water to the same level as the syrup in the bottles. Bring the water to simmering point, 88°C/190°F and hold for 20 minutes or heat the water to 77°C/170°F and hold for 30 minutes. Remove the bottles and secure the tops. When cold seal the corks by dipping in melted paraffin wax.
Chemical process: this is an easier method but has a bleaching effect on the colour of the fruit and a slight sulphur flavour which is harmless. Crush 1 tablet and dissolve in 1 × 15 ml spoon/1 tablespoon warm water, then stir into 600 ml/1 pint syrup or juice before pouring

into the bottle. Seal well.

The juice will keep for about six months.

LIQUEURS

Extravagant but delicious, fruits can be infused with spirits for several days or weeks before bottling and no sterilizing is necessary. The steeped fruits may be used for desserts.

EQUIPMENT NEEDED

A fruit squeezer, liquidizer or juice extractor, bottles, funnel for pouring, sieve, deep saucepan for sterilizing bottles, and paraffin wax for sealing corks.

Fresh bitter lemon

Metric	Imperial
500 g (about 4) lemons	1 lb (about 4) lemons
100 g granulated sugar	4 oz granulated sugar
600 ml water	1 pint water

Thinly pare the lemons, then place the peel in a liquidizer goblet. Remove the pith. Cut the lemons in half and place in the goblet. Add the sugar and half the water. Blend at high speed for 1 minute, then strain.

Return the pulp to the goblet and pour over the remaining water. Blend again for 1 minute, then strain and add to the first strained juice. Pour into prepared bottles, leaving 1–2.5 cm/½–1 inch headspace. Sterilize with the heat process or Campden solution.

Makes about 1¼ litres/2¼ pints

Tomato juice

Fresh bitter lemon;
Tomato juice

Metric	Imperial
1¾ kg tomatoes, quartered	4 lb tomatoes, quartered
2 onions, peeled and chopped	2 onions, peeled and chopped
8 sprigs of mint	8 sprigs of mint
1 × 15 ml spoon sugar	1 tablespoon sugar
1 × 5 ml spoon salt	1 teaspoon salt
1 × 1.25 ml spoon pepper	¼ teaspoon pepper
1.2 litres water	2 pints water
grated rind and juice of 2 lemons	grated rind and juice of 2 lemons

Cooking time: about 30 minutes

Place all the ingredients, except the lemon juice, in a saucepan. Cover the pan and bring to the boil. Reduce the heat, then simmer for 10 to 15 minutes, or until the tomatoes are soft.

Liquidize and sieve the mixture, or rub through a sieve to give a thick juice. Return the juice to a pan, add the lemon juice and bring to the boil. Taste and adjust the seasoning and adjust the consistency with more water, if liked. Pour into prepared bottles, leaving 1–2.5 cm/½–1 inch headspace. Sterilize with the heat process.

Makes about 2¼ litres/4 pints

Black currant syrup

Metric	Imperial
1¾ kg black currants	4 lb black currants
grated rind and juice of 2 oranges	grated rind and juice of 2 oranges
1.2 litres water	2 pints water
approx 750 g sugar	approx 1½ lb sugar

Cooking time: about 3 minutes

Wash the currants and place in a saucepan with the orange rind and juice. Pour the water over them, then bring to the boil, stirring. Boil for 1 minute, crushing the currants well with a wooden spoon. Strain the juice through a sieve or jelly bag, pressing the pulp well.

Measure the juice and add 350 g/12 oz sugar for every 600 ml/1 pint juice. Stir well until the sugar is completely dissolved, heating gently if necessary. Pour the syrup into prepared bottles, leaving 1–2.5 cm/½–1 inch headspace. Sterilize with the heat process or Campden solution.
Makes about 1¾ litres/3 pints

Variation:
Substitute red currants for the black currants.

Lemon syrup

Metric	Imperial
grated rind and juice of 1 kg (about 8) lemons	grated rind and juice of 2 lb (about 8) lemons
grated rind and juice of 2 oranges	grated rind and juice of 2 oranges
1 kg granulated sugar	2 lb granulated sugar
1.2 litres water	2 pints water
2 × 15 ml spoons citric acid	2 tablespoons citric acid

Cooking time: about 10 minutes

Put the grated rinds into a large saucepan. Add the sugar and water and bring to the boil slowly, stirring to dissolve the sugar.
Pour the squeezed fruit juices into a large heatproof bowl or jug. Pour on the boiling syrup, then stir in the citric acid. Leave to cool. Strain and pour into prepared bottles, leaving 1–2.5 cm/½–1 inch headspace. Sterilize with the heat process or Campden solution.
Makes about 2 litres/3½ pints

Variations:
Substitute oranges, limes or grapefruit for the lemons, and use lemons instead of the oranges.

Strawberry syrup

Metric	Imperial
1¾ kg strawberries	4 lb strawberries
approx 750 g sugar	approx 1½ lb sugar
approx 3 × 5 ml spoons lemon juice	approx 3 teaspoons lemon juice

Place the berries in a jar or bowl and crush well with a wooden spoon. Cover and leave for about 1 day in a warm room, until the fruit begins to ferment, when bubbles will form on the surface.
Alternatively the juice may be extracted by placing the raspberries in a basin over a pan of boiling water, then crushing until the juice runs. Or heat the berries directly in a saucepan. Bring to the boil, then cook for 1 minute, crushing the fruit.
For either method, strain the juice through a jelly bag or sieve. Add 225–350 g/8–12 oz sugar and 5 ml/1 teaspoon lemon juice for each 600 ml/1 pint juice. Stir until the sugar is dissolved, heating gently if necessary. Pour the syrup into prepared bottles, leaving 1–2.5 cm/½–1 inch headspace. Sterilize with the heat process.
Makes about 1¾ litres/3 pints

Variation:
Substitute raspberries, blackberries, loganberries or mulberries for the strawberries.

Left: Black currant syrup
Right: Strawberry syrup; Ginger syrup; Lemon syrup

Ginger syrup

Metric	Imperial
225 g root ginger	½ lb root ginger
1 kg sugar	2 lb sugar
1 litre water	1¾ pints water
1 cinnamon stick	1 cinnamon stick
grated rind and juice of	grated rind and juice of
1 lemon	1 lemon

Cooking time: about 1¼ hours

Scrub well or peel the root ginger. Cut into thin slices, then roughly chop it. Place it in a saucepan with the sugar, water, cinnamon and lemon rind and juice.

Bring to the boil slowly, stirring until the sugar dissolves. Reduce the heat, cover the pan, then simmer for 1 hour or until syrupy. Strain and pour the syrup into prepared bottles, leaving 1–2.5 cm/½–1 inch headspace. Sterilize with the heat process.

Makes about 1½ litres/2½ pints

Spiced blackberry cordial

Spiced blackberry cordial

Metric
1¾ kg blackberries
600 ml water
1 × 15 ml spoon whole
  cloves
1 × 15 ml spoon grated
  nutmeg
2 cinnamon sticks
approx 500 g sugar
300 ml brandy

Imperial
4 lb blackberries
1 pint water
1 tablespoon whole
  cloves
1 tablespoon grated
  nutmeg
2 cinnamon sticks
approx 1 lb sugar
½ pint brandy

Cooking time: about 20 minutes

Place the blackberries in a pan with the water and spices. Cover and bring to the boil. Reduce the heat, then simmer for 15 minutes or until the blackberries are soft.
Strain through a sieve or muslin and measure the juice. For every 600 ml/1 pint juice add 500 g/1 lb sugar and stir until dissolved. If necessary, heat gently to dissolve the sugar, then stir in the brandy. Pour into prepared bottles, straining to remove seeds if necessary.
Makes about 1¾ litres/3 pints

Sloe gin

Metric
500 g sloe berries
100 g sugar
1 litre gin
2 × 15 ml spoons
  split almonds

Imperial
1 lb sloe berries
4 oz sugar
1¾ pints gin
2 tablespoons
  split almonds

The task of pricking sloes may be speeded up by making your own sloe-pricker. Slice a piece of cork to about 1 cm/½ inch thickness, then stick sewing pins through it. Place the sloes on a tray and prick them all over.

Remove the stalks from the sloes, then prick the sloes well. Place in a jar with the sugar and almonds. Pour in the gin. Seal the jar, then shake well to dissolve the sugar and distribute the berries. Leave in a cool dark place for 3 months, shaking the bottle occasionally. The sloes may be kept in the gin, or strained off and eaten separately. Bottle the gin.
Makes about 1.2 litres/2 pints

Variations:
Substitute damsons for the sloes, or use raspberries or red or black currants which will not need pricking.

Orange whisky

Metric	Imperial
2 oranges	2 oranges
100 g sugar	4 oz sugar
1 × 5 ml spoon coriander seeds	1 teaspoon coriander seeds
600 ml whisky	1 pint whisky

Thinly peel the rind from the oranges. Cut the rind into thin strips and place in a jar. Squeeze the juice, and add to the jar with the sugar and coriander seeds. Pour in the whisky, then seal the bottle. Shake to dissolve the sugar and distribute the flavour. Leave in a cool dark place for 1 to 2 months, shaking the bottle occasionally. Strain and bottle the whisky.
Makes 750 ml/1¼ pints

From left: Cherry brandy; Orange whisky; Sloe gin

Cherry brandy

Metric	Imperial
500 g cherries	1 lb cherries
225 g caster sugar	8 oz caster sugar
2 × 15 ml spoons split almonds	2 tablespoons split almonds
1 cinnamon stick	1 cinnamon stick
2 cloves	2 cloves
600 ml brandy	1 pint brandy

Wash and dry the cherries. Trim or remove the stalks and prick the cherries in several places with a cocktail stick. Place the cherries in a jar with the sugar, almonds and spices. Pour in the brandy, then seal the jar. Shake well to dissolve the sugar and distribute the flavours.
Leave in a dark place for 3 months. Shake the bottle several times a week, until the brandy is a rich cherry colour. Strain off the cherries and eat them separately. Bottle the brandy.
Makes about 900 ml/1½ pints

PICKLES

Pickles are made from raw or lightly cooked fruit and vegetables preserved in vinegar with the addition of sugar, salt and spices.

Vegetables for pickling are first brined (layered with salt or steeped in a brine solution) for 24 hours. This helps to extract water which would otherwise dilute the vinegar and therefore reduce its preservative quality; salt also helps to make the vegetables crisp.

Fruits for pickling are usually lightly cooked before pickling in sweetened vinegar.

All these pickles keep for up to 1 year.

PREPARING FRUIT AND VEGETABLES
Use young, fresh fruit and vegetables, removing any damaged parts. Wash and drain well, then peel, trim and cut up as necessary.

BRINING
Brining can be done in two ways: wet or dry.
Wet brining: place the whole or cut up vegetables in a large bowl and pour over a brine solution, place a plate on top so that the vegetables are completely immersed in the solution. A solution of 50 g/2 oz of salt to every 600 ml/1 pint water is sufficient to brine 500 g/1 lb vegetables.
Dry brining: use this method for vegetables containing a lot of water such as marrow and cucumber. Layer the vegetables with salt in a large bowl, cover and leave for 24 hours. Allow 25 to 50 g/1 to 2 oz salt for every 50 g/1 lb vegetables. (1 × 15 ml spoon/1 tablespoon salt equals about 1 oz.) Drain off the salt water, rinse and drain the vegetables well.

FILLING THE JARS
Neatly pack the dried fruit or vegetables tightly into clean dry jars, right to the neck, but without bruising or squashing them. Any excess water in the jar can be drained out.

Pour flavoured vinegar over the vegetables or fruit to cover completely. The vinegar may be hot or cold, the latter giving a crisper pickle. Any type of vinegar may be used – malt, distilled, wine or cider vinegars – as long as it has an acetic acid content of at least 5 per cent; special pickling malt vinegar of 8 per cent acetic acid strength is available. Flavour the vinegar with whole herbs and spices.

COVERING THE JARS
It is very important that pickles should be covered with air-tight, vinegar-proof lids. Vinegar corrodes bare metal which would taint and discolour a pickle, and it would also evaporate through jam covers and greaseproof paper if used, causing a pickle to dry out.

Metal screw-tops with plastic-coated linings such as are used for coffee jars and commercially prepared pickle jars are ideal. Otherwise use plastic tops or Porosan preserving skin or bottling jars. Corks may be used if they are first boiled, fit the jar well so they are airtight and are tied down with greaseproof paper.

EQUIPMENT NEEDED
For making pickles you need a preserving pan or large saucepan; this must *not* be made of brass, copper or iron as vinegar corrodes these metals. Aluminium, stainless steel and unchipped aluminium coated pans are perfect. You will also need heat-proof, wide-necked jars with airtight, vinegar-proof covers, and a large bowl to hold the vegetables in brine.

Flavoured vinegars

For the best pickles, the vinegar should be flavoured with spices or herbs. Whole spices and whole fresh herbs should be used to keep the vinegar clear. Vinegar may be bought already spiced, or you may buy ready-made pickling spice, but it is more fun to mix your own spices. You can use malt vinegar, or red or white wine vinegar which will give a more refined flavour.

Herb vinegars

Half fill a bottle with sprigs or leaves of fresh herbs. Use either mixed or one variety, e.g. parsley, thyme, sage, tarragon, rosemary or mint. Fill up the bottle with the best vinegar, preferably red or white wine vinegar. Seal the bottle and leave to steep for at least 2 weeks. Strain before using.

Herb vinegars can also be used to add flavour to vinaigrette and mayonnaise dressings. Tarragon vinegar is traditionally used to flavour bearnaise sauce.

Basic spiced vinegar; Herb vinegars; Basic vegetable pickle

Basic spiced vinegar

Metric	Imperial
1 litre vinegar	2 pints vinegar
5 cm cinnamon stick	2 inch cinnamon stick
1 × 15 ml spoon cloves	1 tablespoon cloves
1 × 15 ml spoon mace blades	1 tablespoon mace blades
1 × 15 ml spoon allspice berries	1 tablespoon allspice berries
1 × 15 ml spoon peppercorns	1 tablespoon peppercorns
2 bay leaves	2 bay leaves

Vinegar may be spiced in two different ways.

Method 1 : Put all the flavourings in a bottle and pour in the vinegar. Seal, then leave for 1 to 2 months, shaking the bottle occasionally. This gives the finest results.

Method 2 : To spice vinegar quickly, place the vinegar and spices in a saucepan, cover and bring up to boiling point. Remove from the heat and leave to steep for 2 to 3 hours, then strain.

Variation :

For a hot spiced vinegar, add 1 × 15 ml spoon/1 tablespoon dried chillies and 2 × 15 ml spoons/2 tablespoons mustard seed. 1 × 15 ml spoon/1 tablespoon fennel or dill seeds may also be added.

Mixed vegetable pickle

Metric	Imperial
1½ kg mixed vegetables (e.g. onions, cauliflower, cucumber, courgettes, beans, tomatoes, carrots)	3 lb mixed vegetables (e.g. onions, cauliflower, cucumber, courgettes, beans, tomatoes, carrots)
75 g (3 × 15 ml spoons) salt or brine of 175 g salt and 1¾ litres water	3 oz (3 tablespoons) salt or brine of 6 oz salt and 3 pints water
750 ml to 1 litre spiced vinegar	1¼ to 1¾ pints spiced vinegar

Prepare the vegetables by peeling if necessary, then cut into slices, dice or small pieces. Place in a large bowl and either layer with salt or steep in brine solution. Cover and leave for 24 hours to extract the moisture from the vegetables.

Rinse the vegetables well to remove the excess salt, drain and dry well. Pack into prepared jars and cover with enough hot or cold spiced vinegar to cover the vegetables completely. Seal with airtight, vinegar-proof covers.

Makes about 1½ kg/3 lb

Pickled eggs

Metric	Imperial
450 ml vinegar	¾ pint vinegar
1 × 2.5 ml spoon salt	½ teaspoon salt
1 × 5 ml spoon black peppercorns	1 teaspoon black peppercorns
1 × 5 ml spoon allspice berries	1 teaspoon allspice berries
15 g root ginger, peeled and cut into matchsticks	½ oz root ginger, peeled and cut into matchsticks
12 small eggs	12 small eggs
sprigs of fresh herbs e.g. thyme, parsley, tarragon (optional)	sprigs of fresh herbs e.g. thyme, parsley, tarragon (optional)

Choose either malt, distilled, red or white wine vinegar to give different flavours and colour effects. Use a wide-necked jar.

Pour the vinegar into a saucepan. Add the salt, peppercorns, allspice and ginger and bring to the boil. Simmer for 2 minutes, then leave to cool. Meanwhile hard-boil the eggs for at least 10 minutes, then place them in a bowl of cold water to cool. When cold, carefully peel off the shells.

Place the eggs in prepared jars, leaving enough space for the vinegar to completely cover all the eggs. Pieces of egg not in contact with the vinegar will remain white and therefore give a mottled appearance.

Pour in the cold spiced vinegar to cover all the eggs. The spices may be added to the jar for a spicier taste, or they may be strained off. Sprigs of fresh herbs may also be added to the jar to give a herb flavour and an attractive appearance. Seal with air-tight, vinegar-proof covers.

Makes 1 kg/2 lb (12 pickled eggs)

Top shelf: Pickled eggs in red and white wine vinegar; Pickled shallots. Bottom shelf: Pickled shallots; Pickled eggs in malt vinegar; Cucumber pickle

Pickled shallots

Metric	Imperial
1 kg shallots	2 lb shallots
100 g salt	4 oz salt
1.2 litres water	2 pints water
900 ml spiced malt vinegar (page 69)	1½ pints spiced malt vinegar (page 69)

Small pickling onions may also be pickled in this way. Use a wide-necked jar.

Place the unpeeled shallots in a bowl (they are easier to peel after brining). Mix the salt with the water and pour it over the shallots. Place a plate on top of the shallots to ensure they are immersed in the brine. Leave for 24 hours to extract the moisture.
Drain the shallots, then peel. Rinse them well and dry them. Pour the spiced vinegar into a large saucepan and bring to the boil. Add the shallots, return to the boil and simmer for 1 minute. Drain the shallots, reserving the vinegar, then pack them into prepared jars. Pour over the vinegar to cover the shallots. Seal with airtight, vinegar-proof covers.
Makes 1½ kg/3 lb

Cucumber pickle

Metric	Imperial
1 kg (2 large) cucumbers	2 lb (2 large) cucumbers
2 onions, peeled and thinly sliced	2 onions, peeled and thinly sliced
1 green pepper, quartered, cored, seeded, and thinly sliced	1 green pepper, quartered, cored, seeded, and thinly sliced
3 × 15 ml spoons salt	3 tablespoons salt
450 ml cider vinegar	¾ pint cider vinegar
225 g granulated sugar	8 oz granulated sugar
2 × 15 ml spoons mustard seed	2 tablespoons mustard seed
1 × 5 ml spoon ground ginger	1 teaspoon ground ginger

Cooking time: about 10 minutes

Cut the cucumbers into 5 mm/¼ inch slices and place in a bowl with the onion and pepper. Sprinkle with the salt, cover and leave for 12 hours to extract the moisture. Rinse the vegetables well to remove the salt, then drain and dry well.
Place the vinegar in a large saucepan with the remaining ingredients, heat slowly until the sugar dissolves, then bring to the boil. Add the vegetables and simmer gently for 5 minutes or until the vegetables are just tender. Spoon the pickle into prepared jars and pour in the remaining vinegar. Seal with airtight, vinegar-proof covers.
Makes 2 kg/4½ lb

Pickled beetroot with lemon; Pickled mushrooms;
Pickled red cabbage; Pickled artichokes

Pickled beetroot with lemon

Metric
450 ml distilled white
   vinegar
2 lemons, thinly sliced,
   pips and ends removed
2 onions, peeled and
   thinly sliced
2 × 15 ml spoons
   granulated sugar
1 cinnamon stick
1 kg beetroot, cooked

Imperial
¾ pint distilled white
   vinegar
2 lemons, thinly sliced,
   pips and ends removed
2 onions, peeled and
   thinly sliced
2 tablespoons
   granulated sugar
1 cinnamon stick
2 lb beetroot, cooked

Cooking time: about 5 minutes

Use a wide-necked jar for this pickle.

Pour the vinegar into a saucepan and add the remaining ingredients except the beetroot. Bring to the boil and simmer for 1 minute. Strain the lemons and onions, reserving the vinegar. Peel the cooked beetroots and cut them into thin slices.
Pack the beetroot into prepared jars, making occasional layers of onion and lemon slices. Pour in the vinegar to cover the beetroot. Seal with airtight, vinegar-proof covers.
Makes 1½ kg/3 lb

Pickled mushrooms

Metric
500 g small firm
   button mushrooms
300 ml malt vinegar
1 shallot, peeled and finely
   chopped
1 × 15 ml spoon finely
   chopped root ginger
2 mace blades
1 × 5 ml spoon salt
1 × 2.5 ml spoon ground
   black pepper
4 sprigs of thyme
4 × 15 ml spoons sherry

Imperial
1 lb small firm
   button mushrooms
½ pint malt vinegar
1 shallot, peeled and finely
   chopped
1 tablespoon finely
   chopped root ginger
2 mace blades
1 teaspoon salt
½ teaspoon ground
   black pepper
4 sprigs of thyme
4 tablespoons sherry

Cooking time: about 15 minutes

Clean the mushrooms well, washing them if necessary and drying them well. Trim the stalks. Pour the vinegar into a pan and add the remaining ingredients except the sherry. Bring to the boil and simmer for 5 minutes. Add the mushrooms to the boiling vinegar, then return to the boil. Cover the pan and simmer for 1 minute until the mushrooms have shrunk slightly. Stir in the sherry. Spoon the mushrooms into a prepared jar and pour in the hot vinegar. Seal with airtight, vinegar-proof covers.
Makes 500 g/1¼ lb

Pickled red cabbage

Metric	Imperial
1 kg (1 medium) red cabbage	2 lb (1 medium) red cabbage
2 × 15 ml spoons salt	2 tablespoons salt
600 ml spiced malt vinegar (page 69)	1 pint spiced malt vinegar (page 69)
2 large oranges	2 large oranges
1 large onion, peeled and thinly sliced	1 large onion, peeled and thinly sliced
50 g raisins	2 oz raisins
1 × 15 ml spoon soft brown sugar	1 tablespoon soft brown sugar

Cooking time: about 5 minutes

Remove any limp outside leaves from the cabbage. Cut the cabbage into quarters using a stainless steel knife to prevent discoloration. Remove and discard the hard central core, and shred the rest finely. Place it in a large bowl, layering with the salt. Cover and leave for 24 hours to extract the moisture. Rinse well to remove the salt, then drain and dry well.
Pour the vinegar into a saucepan. Grate the rind from the oranges, peel and discard the pith, then cut the flesh into segments. Add the orange rind and flesh and remaining ingredients to the pan and bring to the boil.
Place the cabbage in a large bowl, pour the hot vinegar mixture over it and mix well. If the cabbage has turned a purple-blue colour it will turn red again on mixing with the vinegar. Pack the cabbage into prepared jars and pour in the remaining vinegar to cover the cabbage. Seal with airtight, vinegar-proof covers.
Makes 1¾ kg/4 lb

Pickled artichokes

Metric	Imperial
1 kg Jerusalem artichokes	2 lb Jerusalem artichokes
1 × 2.5 ml spoon salt	½ teaspoon salt
600 ml distilled white vinegar	1 pint distilled white vinegar
1 lemon	1 lemon
2 sprigs of parsley	2 sprigs of parsley
2 sprigs of thyme	2 sprigs of thyme
2 bay leaves	2 bay leaves

Cooking time: about 45 minutes

Wash the artichokes but do not peel them. Place them in a saucepan, cover with cold water and add the salt. Cover the pan, bring to the boil and simmer for 15 to 20 minutes or until the artichokes are just tender and the skin peels away with a knife. Drain and leave until cool enough to handle, then peel them.
Meanwhile, prepare the flavoured vinegar. Place the vinegar in a large saucepan. Thinly pare the lemon and cut the peel into thin strips. Squeeze the juice from the lemon into the vinegar with the strips of lemon peel. Add the remaining ingredients and bring to the boil, then remove from the heat.
Cut the artichokes into round slices, about 5 mm/¼ inch thick. Add them immediately to the pan of flavoured vinegar to prevent discoloration. Return to the boil and simmer for 10 minutes until tender but not soft. With a slotted spoon pack the artichokes into prepared jars. Pour in the flavoured vinegar to cover the artichokes completely. Seal with airtight, vinegar-proof covers.
Makes 1½ kg/3¼ lb

Underground pickle

Underground pickle

Metric
500 g carrots, peeled
and cut into sticks
(about 3 cm × 5 mm)
225 g parsnips, peeled
and cut into sticks
(about 3 cm × 5 mm)
225 g turnips, peeled
and cut into 1 cm
square cubes
225 g celery, washed
and cut into slices
about 1 cm thick
225 g onions, peeled
and sliced
3 × 15 ml spoons salt
1 litre malt vinegar
225 g soft brown sugar
1 large garlic clove,
peeled and crushed
25 g root ginger,
peeled and thinly sliced
2 bay leaves
1 × 15 ml spoon mustard
seeds
1 × 15 ml spoon fennel seeds
1 × 5 ml spoon allspice
berries
1 × 5 ml spoon black
peppercorns

Imperial
1 lb carrots, peeled
and cut into sticks
(about 1¼ × ¼ inch)
8 oz parsnips, peeled
and cut into sticks
(about 1¼ × ¼ inch)
8 oz turnips, peeled
and cut into ½ inch
square cubes
8 oz celery, washed
and cut into slices
about ½ inch thick
8 oz onions, peeled
and sliced
3 tablespoons salt
1¾ pints malt vinegar
8 oz soft brown sugar
1 large garlic clove,
peeled and crushed
1 oz root ginger,
peeled and thinly sliced
2 bay leaves
1 tablespoon mustard
seeds
1 tablespoon fennel seeds
1 teaspoon allspice
berries
1 teaspoon black
peppercorns

Place the vegetables in a large bowl, sprinkling each layer with the salt. Cover and leave for 12 hours to extract the excess moisture. Rinse well to remove the salt, then drain and dry well. Place the vinegar in a saucepan with the remaining ingredients. Heat slowly to dissolve the sugar, then bring to the boil and remove from the heat.

Meanwhile pack the vegetables loosely into prepared jars, allowing enough space for the vinegar and spices to surround all the vegetables. Pour in the hot vinegar and push the whole spices down the side of the jar. Seal the jars with airtight, vinegar-proof covers.

Makes 2½ kg/5½ lb

Honey spiced orange pickle

Metric
1 kg (6 medium) oranges
300 ml malt vinegar
500 g clear honey
1 cinnamon stick
1 × 2.5 ml spoon cloves
1 × 2.5 ml spoon
   peppercorns
1 × 5 ml spoon coriander
   seeds
1 × 5 ml spoon cardamom
   pods

Imperial
2¼ lb (6 medium) oranges
½ pint malt vinegar
1 lb clear honey
1 cinnamon stick
½ teaspoon cloves
½ teaspoon
   peppercorns
1 teaspoon coriander
   seeds
1 teaspoon cardamom
   pods

Cooking time: about 1¼ hours

Place the oranges in a saucepan and cover with salted water. Bring to the boil and simmer for 45 minutes to 1 hour until tender. Drain and cool. Slice the oranges thinly and discard the pips. Pour the vinegar into a saucepan and add the remaining ingredients. Heat slowly, stirring to dissolve the honey, then bring to the boil. Simmer for 10 minutes.

Place the sliced oranges in a large saucepan and strain over the hot vinegar mixture. Return to the boil and simmer for 15 minutes, stirring frequently. Spoon into prepared jars and pour the vinegar over to cover. Seal with airtight, vinegar-proof covers.

Makes about 1½ kg/3¼ lb

Spiced pickled pears

Metric
450 ml red wine vinegar
500 g granulated sugar
grated rind of 1 lemon
1 × 15 ml spoon peeled
   and finely chopped
   root ginger
1 cinnamon stick
1 × 5 ml spoon cloves
1½ kg cooking pears

Imperial
¾ pint red wine vinegar
1 lb granulated sugar
grated rind of 1 lemon
1 tablespoon peeled
   and finely chopped
   root ginger
1 cinnamon stick
1 teaspoon cloves
3 lb cooking pears

Cooking time: about 20 minutes

Use a wide-necked preserving jar.

Place all the ingredients except the pears in a large saucepan. Heat slowly, stirring to dissolve the sugar, then bring to the boil. Peel the pears, cut into quarters and remove the cores. Thickly slice the pears and add to the pan. Cook gently for about 5 minutes or until the pears are just tender but not soft. Carefully remove the pears with a slotted spoon and pack them into prepared jars; arranging the slices across for the best effect. The spices may be discarded or added to the pears in the jar for a stronger flavour. Boil the remaining vinegar mixture until thickened to a syrup, about 450 ml/¾ pint. Pour the vinegar syrup over the pears to cover them. Seal with airtight, vinegar-proof covers.

Makes 1 kg/2 lb

Honey spiced orange pickle; Spiced pickled pears

Pickled peppers

Metric	Imperial
1½ kg peppers, red or green or a mixture of both	3 lb peppers, red or green or a mixture of both
3 × 15 ml spoons salt	3 tablespoons salt
750 ml red wine vinegar	1¼ pints red wine vinegar
2 bay leaves	2 bay leaves
2 sprigs of thyme	2 sprigs of thyme
2 sprigs of parsley	2 sprigs of parsley
1 × 5 ml spoon peppercorns	1 teaspoon peppercorns

Cooking time: 5 minutes

Cut the peppers into halves or quarters, depending on their size. Remove the seeds and core and cut into 5 mm/¼ inch thick slices. Place in a bowl, sprinkling each layer with the salt. Cover and leave for 12 hours to extract the moisture. Rinse the peppers well to remove the salt, then drain and dry well.
Place the vinegar in a saucepan with the remaining ingredients, tied in a muslin bag if just the flavour is required. Heat the vinegar to boiling point. Meanwhile pack the peppers into prepared jars, then strain in the hot flavoured vinegar. Position the herbs down the sides of the jars to look attractive. Seal the jars with airtight, vinegar-proof covers.
Makes 1¾ kg/4 lb

Pickled French beans

Metric	Imperial
900 ml white wine vinegar	1½ pints white wine vinegar
1 onion, peeled and thinly sliced	1 onion, peeled and thinly sliced
1 × 5 ml spoon salt	1 teaspoon salt
2 × 15 ml spoons granulated sugar	1 tablespoon granulated sugar
1 × 5 ml spoon white peppercorns	1 teaspoon white peppercorns
1 × 5 ml spoon coriander seeds	1 teaspoon coriander seeds
1 × 15 ml spoon all-spice berries	1 tablespoon all-spice berries
2 bay leaves	2 bay leaves
500 g French beans, topped and tailed	1 lb French beans, topped and tailed

Cooking time: about 15 minutes

Use a wide-necked jar for this pickle.

Pour the vinegar into a large saucepan and add all the ingredients except the beans. Bring to the boil and simmer for 5 minutes. Add the beans, return to the boil, cover and simmer for about 5 minutes or until the beans are just tender but still crisp.
Drain the beans, reserving the vinegar. Pack the beans in upright bundles into prepared jars. Pour in the vinegar, straining off the flavourings. Seal with airtight, vinegar-proof covers.
Makes 1¼ kg/2½ lb

Ingredients for Pickled peppers, Pickled French beans and Pickled black eyed peas

Pickled peppers; Pickled black eyed peas; Pickled French beans

Pickled black eyed peas

Metric	Imperial
500 g dried black eyed peas	*1 lb dried black eyed peas*
1¾ litres white wine vinegar	*3 pints white wine vinegar*
2 × 15 ml spoons pickling spice	*2 tablespoons pickling spice*
1 onion, peeled and thinly sliced	*1 onion, peeled and thinly sliced*
grated rind and juice of 1 lemon	*grated rind and juice of 1 lemon*
2 × 15 ml spoons soft brown sugar	*2 tablespoons soft brown sugar*
1 × 5 ml spoon salt	*1 teaspoon salt*
1 × 5 ml spoon ground pepper	*1 teaspoon ground pepper*
4 sprigs of thyme	*4 sprigs of thyme*
4 sprigs of parsley	*4 sprigs of parsley*
4 sprigs of marjoram or oregano	*4 sprigs of marjoram or oregano*
2 bay leaves	*2 bay leaves*

Cooking time: About 2 hours 10 minutes

Any dried beans may be substituted for the black eyed peas, e.g. haricot, kidney or butter beans. This pickle is particularly delicious used in salads and hors d'oeuvre.

Place the peas in a bowl. Boil the vinegar with the pickling spice and strain it over the peas while still hot. Cover and leave for at least 2 hours or overnight. Transfer the peas and vinegar to a saucepan and add the remaining ingredients. Cover the pan and bring to the boil. Simmer gently for 2 hours or until the peas are just tender. Spoon the peas with the herbs into prepared jars. Alternatively, for a stronger herb flavour replace the cooked herbs with fresh ones. Pour over the vinegar. Seal with airtight, vinegar-proof covers.

Makes 1¾ kg/4 lb

CHUTNEYS

Chutney is a sweet and sour condiment made from a mixture of fruit and/or vegetables, which are cooked to a pulp with sugar, spices and salt, then mixed with vinegar. The vinegar, salt and spices are the preservatives.

MAKING THE CHUTNEY

The fruit and vegetables are peeled and chopped into small pieces, so slightly over ripe and blemished fruits and vegetables may be used, the damaged parts being discarded. They are then cooked slowly with the vinegar, sugar and flavourings, stirring until the liquid evaporates and the chutney is reduced to a pulp and the consistency of jam (it will thicken slightly on cooling) with no free liquid on the

Irish marrow chutney in preparation (see page 81)

top. Long slow cooking is important to break down fibres and bring out all the flavours; it can take from 1 to 4 hours, but usually 2 hours is long enough, depending on the type of fruit or vegetables used.

Any type of vinegar or sugar may be used, depending on the flavour and colour required for the finished chutney. Even white sugar will give a darkish-coloured chutney if cooked for a long time. So if you want a pale-coloured chutney, add the sugar near the end of the cooking with some of the vinegar. This method can also be used for fruit and vegetables with tough skins as the sugar has a hardening effect.

FILLING AND COVERING THE JARS

Pour the hot chutney into clean, dry, warm jars. The jars should be covered as soon as they are filled and while still hot. Use airtight, vinegar-proof covers as for pickles (see page 68). Clean the jars, label and store in a cool, dry, dark place. Most chutneys taste better on maturing.

EQUIPMENT NEEDED

You need the same items as for making pickles plus a mincer/slicer for preparation of vegetables, a funnel for filling the jars and airtight, vinegar-proof covers.

Mediterranean chutney

Irish marrow chutney

Metric	Imperial
1½ kg marrow, peeled, quartered lengthways, seeded and diced	3 lb marrow, peeled, quartered lengthways, seeded and diced
1½ kg cooking apples, peeled, cored and chopped	3 lb cooking apples, peeled, cored and chopped
225 g onions, peeled and chopped	8 oz onions, peeled and chopped
1 large garlic clove, peeled and crushed	1 large garlic clove, peeled and crushed
100 g sultanas	4 oz sultanas
100 g raisins	4 oz raisins
100 g dried apricots	4 oz dried apricots
100 g preserved ginger, finely chopped or 1 × 15 ml spoon ground ginger	4 oz preserved ginger, finely chopped or 1 tablespoon ground ginger
50 g almonds, blanched and chopped	2 oz almonds, blanched and chopped
4 × 15 ml spoons mustard seeds	4 tablespoons mustard seeds
1 × 15 ml spoon chillies, seeds removed and finely chopped, or ground chilli powder	1 tablespoon chillies, seeds removed and finely chopped, or ground chilli powder
1 × 15 ml spoon salt	1 tablespoon salt
1 × 15 ml spoon ground cinnamon	1 tablespoon ground cinnamon
1 × 5 ml spoon ground cloves	1 teaspoon ground cloves
1 × 5 ml spoon ground nutmeg	1 teaspoon ground nutmeg
900 ml malt vinegar	1½ pints malt vinegar
1¾ kg sugar	4 lb sugar
5 × 15 ml spoons whisky	5 tablespoons whisky

Cooking time: about 2 hours

This chutney is best kept to mature for several months before opening.

Place all the ingredients in a large pan and bring to the boil, stirring. Reduce the heat and simmer for 1½ to 2 hours, stirring occasionally, or until the chutney is thick and the consistency of jam.
Spoon while still hot into prepared jars. Seal with airtight, vinegar-proof covers.
Makes about 3 kg/7 lb

Mediterranean chutney

Metric	Imperial
1 kg tomatoes, skinned and chopped	2 lb tomatoes, skinned and chopped
500 g Spanish onions, peeled and chopped	1 lb Spanish onions, peeled and chopped
500 g courgettes, thinly sliced	1 lb courgettes, thinly sliced
1 large green pepper, cored, seeded and diced	1 large green pepper, cored, seeded and diced
1 large red pepper, cored, seeded and diced	1 large red pepper, cored, seeded and diced
225 g (1 medium) aubergine, diced	8 oz (1 medium) aubergine, diced
2 large garlic cloves, peeled and crushed	2 large garlic cloves, peeled and crushed
1 × 15 ml spoon salt	1 tablespoon salt
1 × 15 ml spoon cayenne pepper	1 tablespoon cayenne pepper
1 × 15 ml spoon paprika pepper	1 tablespoon paprika pepper
1 × 15 ml spoon ground coriander	1 tablespoon ground coriander
300 ml malt vinegar	½ pint malt vinegar
350 g sugar	¾ lb sugar

Cooking time: about 2½ hours

This makes a strong, hot chutney, so leave it for several months to mature, or, if you wish to use it immediately, reduce the amount of cayenne pepper.

Place the tomatoes, onions, courgettes, peppers, aubergine and garlic in a large pan. Add the salt, cayenne and paprika peppers and coriander. Cover and cook gently, stirring occasionally, until the juices run. Bring to the boil, reduce the heat, uncover and simmer for 1 to 1½ hours or until the vegetables are soft but still recognizable as shapes, and most of the water from the tomatoes has evaporated.
Add the vinegar and sugar, stirring to dissolve the sugar. Continue to cook for 1 hour, or until the chutney is thick and there is no free vinegar on the top.
Spoon while still hot into prepared jars. Seal with airtight, vinegar-proof covers.
Makes about 1¾ kg/4 lb

Green tomato chutney

Metric
1¾ kg green tomatoes,
  roughly chopped
500 g cooking apples,
  peeled, cored and
  chopped
500 g onions, peeled and
  chopped
2 large garlic cloves,
  crushed (optional)
225 g sultanas
1 × 15 ml spoon salt
1 × 15 ml spoon pickling
  spice
25 g root ginger, roughly
  chopped
1 chilli
600 ml vinegar
500 g sugar, brown or
  white

Imperial
4 lb green tomatoes,
  roughly chopped
1 lb cooking apples,
  peeled, cored and
  chopped
1 lb onions, peeled
  and chopped
2 large garlic cloves,
  crushed (optional)
8 oz sultanas
1 tablespoon salt
1 tablespoon pickling
  spice
1 oz root ginger,
  roughly chopped
1 chilli
1 pint vinegar
1 lb sugar, brown or
  white

Cooking time: about 2 hours

Unripe, green tomatoes are available at the end of the tomato season, and are often cheaper than ripe tomatoes.

Place the tomatoes, apples and onions in a large pan with the garlic (if using), sultanas and salt. Tie the pickling spice, ginger and chilli in a muslin bag and add to the pan. Add half the vinegar and bring to the boil. Reduce the heat, then simmer for 1 hour or until the vegetables are reduced to a pulp and the mixture is thick.

Dissolve the sugar in the remaining vinegar and add to the chutney. Simmer for about 1½ hours, stirring frequently, or until the chutney is thick.

Remove the muslin bag and spoon while still hot into prepared jars. Seal with airtight, vinegar-proof covers.
Makes about 2½ kg/5½ lb

Irish marrow chutney; Green tomato chutney

Apricot chutney

Metric	Imperial
225 g dried apricots, soaked in water overnight	8 oz dried apricots, soaked in water overnight
500 g cooking apples, peeled, cored and chopped	1 lb cooking apples, peeled, cored and chopped
1 onion, peeled and chopped	1 onion, peeled and chopped
grated rind and juice of 1 lemon or orange	grated rind and juice of 1 lemon or orange
1 × 5 ml spoon salt	1 teaspoon salt
600 ml spiced vinegar (page 69), distilled or malt	1 pint spiced vinegar (page 69), distilled or malt
500 g sugar, white or brown	1 lb sugar, white or brown

Cooking time: about 1¾ hours

Drain the soaked apricots and place in a large pan. Add the remaining ingredients, except for the sugar. Bring to the boil, reduce the heat, then simmer for 45 minutes, or until the fruit is pulpy. Add the sugar, and stir until it is dissolved. Simmer for about 20 minutes until thick.

Spoon while still hot into prepared jars. Seal with airtight, vinegar-proof covers.

Makes about 1¼ kg/2½ lb

Below: Apricot chutney

Spiced peach and orange chutney

Metric	Imperial
1 kg peaches, peeled, quartered and stoned	2 lb peaches, peeled, quartered and stoned
grated rind and juice of 2 oranges	grated rind and juice of 2 oranges
225 g onions, peeled and chopped	8 oz onions, peeled and chopped
225 g sultanas	8 oz sultanas
1 × 15 ml spoon grated root ginger or ground ginger	1 tablespoon grated root ginger or ground ginger
1 × 5 ml spoon ground cinnamon	1 teaspoon ground cinnamon
1 × 5 ml spoon ground allspice	1 teaspoon ground allspice
2 × 5 ml spoons salt	2 teaspoons salt
600 ml wine vinegar	1 pint wine vinegar
225 g granulated sugar	8 oz granulated sugar
100 g flaked almonds	4 oz flaked almonds

Cooking time: about 1¾ hours

Place the peaches in a large pan. Add the remaining ingredients and bring to the boil, stirring. Reduce the heat, then simmer for 1½ hours or until the chutney is thick.

Spoon while still hot into prepared jars. Seal with airtight, vinegar-proof covers.

Makes about 1½ kg/3½ lb

Variation:
Apricots or plums may be substituted for the peaches.

Beetroot chutney

Metric	Imperial
2 kg beetroot, cooked, skinned and diced	4 lb beetroot, cooked, skinned and diced
1 kg cooking apples, peeled, cored and diced	2 lb cooking apples, peeled, cored and diced
500 g onions, peeled and chopped	1 lb onions, peeled and chopped
grated rind and juice of 2 large lemons	grated rind and juice of 2 large lemons
2 × 15 ml spoons grated root ginger or 2 × 5 ml spoons ground ginger	2 tablespoons grated root ginger or 2 teaspoons ground ginger
2 × 5 ml spoons salt	2 teaspoons salt
1 × 5 ml spoon ground pepper	1 teaspoon ground pepper
1 litre vinegar	1¾ pints vinegar
500 g sugar	1 lb sugar

Cooking time: about 2 hours

Place all the ingredients in a large pan. Stir over a low heat until the sugar dissolves. Bring to the boil, reduce the heat and simmer for 1½ hours or until the chutney is thick.

Spoon while still hot into prepared jars. Seal with airtight, vinegar-proof covers.

Makes about 3 kg/7 lb

Spiced peach chutney; Beetroot chutney; Apple and walnut chutney

Apple and walnut chutney

Metric	Imperial
1¾ kg cooking apples, peeled, cored and chopped	4 lb cooking apples, peeled, cored and chopped
1 kg onions, peeled and chopped	2 lb onions, peeled and chopped
grated rind and juice of 2 oranges or lemons	grated rind and juice of 2 oranges or lemons
500 g sultanas	1 lb sultanas
225 g walnuts, chopped	8 oz walnuts, chopped
1 × 15 ml spoon ground ginger	1 tablespoon ground ginger
1 × 15 ml spoon ground cinnamon	1 tablespoon ground cinnamon
1 × 5 ml spoon ground cloves	1 teaspoon ground cloves
1 × 5 ml spoon salt	1 teaspoon salt
1.2 litres cider or malt vinegar	2 pints cider or malt vinegar
500 g brown sugar	1¼ lb brown sugar

Cooking time: about 2¼ hours

Place all the ingredients, except the sugar, in a large pan. Bring to the boil, cover and simmer, stirring occasionally for 1 hour or until the apples are soft. Add the sugar and simmer uncovered for 1 hour, or until the chutney is thick.

Spoon while still hot into prepared jars. Seal with airtight, vinegar-proof covers.

Makes about 3 kg/7 lb

Lemon chutney; Grapefruit chutney

Lemon chutney

Metric	Imperial
1 kg lemons	2 lb lemons
500 g onions, peeled and sliced	1 lb onions, peeled and sliced
500 g sultanas	1 lb sultanas
about 1 litre water	about 2 pints water
3 × 15 ml spoons grated root ginger or 1 × 15 ml spoon ground ginger	3 tablespoons grated root ginger or 1 tablespoon ground ginger
1 × 15 ml spoon salt	1 tablespoon salt
1 × 5 ml spoon cayenne pepper	1 teaspoon cayenne pepper
600 ml vinegar	1 pint vinegar
750 g soft brown sugar	1½ lb soft brown sugar
4 × 15 ml spoons mustard seed	4 tablespoons mustard seed
2 chillies	2 chillies

Cooking time: about 2 hours

This chutney is made like a lemon marmalade; by softening the peel, then adding the sugar and vinegar and cooking until thick.

Wash the lemons, cut in half and squeeze out the juice. Cut in half again, then cut into shreds (as for marmalade). Place the lemon shreds in a pan with the onion and sultanas. Cover with water, bring to the boil, cover and simmer for 1 hour or until tender.
Alternatively, cook in a pressure cooker with half the amount of water for 10 minutes at high pressure, then reduce the pressure slowly.
Drain off the water, then place the lemon, onion and sultanas in a large pan. Add the remaining ingredients. Stir over a low heat until the sugar dissolves. Bring to the boil, reduce the heat, then simmer for 1 hour, or until the chutney is thick.
Remove the chillies and spoon while still hot into prepared jars. Seal with airtight, vinegar-proof covers.
Makes about 2¼ kg/5 lb

Variation:
Omit the chillies for a milder chutney.

Grapefruit chutney

Metric	Imperial
1½ kg (4 large) grapefruit	3 lb (4 large) grapefruit
1 kg onions, peeled and sliced	2 lb onions, peeled and sliced
about 1 litre water	about 1¾ pints water
225 g sultanas	8 oz sultanas
225 g hazelnuts, skinned	8 oz hazelnuts, skinned
2 × 5 ml spoons ground ginger	2 teaspoons ground ginger
2 × 5 ml spoons salt	2 teaspoons salt
1 litre white wine vinegar	1¾ pints white wine vinegar
750 g granulated sugar	1¾ lb granulated sugar

Cooking time: about 1½ hours

This is a mild chutney, with a distinct flavour of grapefruit. It may be eaten almost immediately after making.

Wash the grapefruit. Peel thinly with a potato peeler. Cut the rind into strips, then place in a saucepan with the onions. Just cover with water, bring to the boil and simmer for 15 minutes. Drain off the water and return the grapefruit rind and onion to a large pan.
Cut the pith away from the grapefruit with a sharp knife. Cut the grapefruit into segments, discarding the membrane and pips, then add to the pan. Add the remaining ingredients.
Bring to the boil, stirring until the sugar dissolves. Reduce the heat, then simmer for 1 hour, or until the fruit is soft and the chutney is thick.
Spoon while still hot into prepared jars. Seal with airtight, vinegar-proof covers.
Makes about 2 kg/4½ lb

From left: Spiced rhubarb and orange chutney; Pear and ginger chutney

Spiced rhubarb and orange chutney

Metric
1½ kg rhubarb, sliced
500 g onions, peeled
   and chopped
4 large oranges
1 × 15 ml spoon mixed
   spice
1 × 15 ml spoon ground
   ginger
1 × 5 ml spoon salt
600 ml wine vinegar
500 g sugar, brown
   or white

Imperial
3 lb rhubarb, sliced
1 lb onions, peeled
   and chopped
4 large oranges
1 tablespoon mixed
   spice
1 tablespoon ground
   ginger
1 teaspoon salt
1 pint wine vinegar
1 lb sugar, brown
   or white

Cooking time: about 2 hours

Place the rhubarb and onion in a large pan. Thinly peel the rind from the oranges with a potato peeler. Cut the rind into thin strips and add to the pan. Squeeze the juice from the oranges and add to the pan.
Add the mixed spice, ginger and salt and half the vinegar, and cook gently for 1 hour, or until the fruit is soft and the mixture thickened. Add the remaining vinegar with the sugar, stirring until the sugar dissolves. Simmer for 45 minutes or until thick.
Spoon while still hot into prepared jars. Seal with airtight, vinegar-proof covers.
Makes about 1¾ kg/4 lb

Pear and ginger chutney

Metric
25 g root ginger,
   roughly chopped
1 × 5 ml spoon cloves
2¾ kg pears, peeled,
   cored and chopped
500 g onions, peeled
   and chopped
100 g stem ginger,
   finely chopped
grated rind and juice
   of 3 oranges
750 g granulated sugar
900 ml red wine vinegar

Imperial
1 oz root ginger,
   roughly chopped
1 teaspoon cloves
6 lb pears, peeled,
   cored and chopped
1 lb onions, peeled
   and chopped
4 oz stem ginger,
   finely chopped
grated rind and juice
   of 3 oranges
1½ lb granulated sugar
1½ pints red wine vinegar

Cooking time: about 2 hours

Tie the root ginger and cloves in a muslin bag, then place all the ingredients in a large pan. Stir over a low heat until the sugar dissolves. Bring to the boil, reduce the heat and simmer for 1½ hours or until the chutney is thick.
Remove the muslin bag and spoon while still hot into prepared jars. Seal with airtight, vinegar-proof covers.
Makes about 1¾ kg/4 lb

Uncooked chutney; Minted blackberry and apple chutney;
Banana and date chutney; Mint chutney

Uncooked chutney

Metric	Imperial
500 g mixed dried fruit (e.g. apricot, prune, apple, fig, pear)	1 lb mixed dried fruit (e.g. apricot, prune, apple, fig, pear)
600 ml spiced malt vinegar (page 69)	1 pint spiced malt vinegar (page 69)
500 g cooking apples, peeled and cored	1 lb cooking apples, peeled and cored
500 g onions, peeled and roughly chopped	1 lb onions, peeled and roughly chopped
grated rind and juice of 1 orange	grated rind and juice of 1 orange
1 × 5 ml spoon salt	1 teaspoon salt
500g soft brown sugar	1 lb soft brown sugar

Soak the dried fruit in the vinegar overnight. Drain, reserving the vinegar, and stone the prunes. Mince the dried fruit with the apples and onions and place in a large bowl. Add the reserved vinegar, orange rind and juice, salt and sugar and stir well to mix. Cover and leave for 24 hours, stirring occasionally, until the sugar is dissolved.
Spoon into prepared jars and seal with airtight, vinegar-proof covers.
Makes about 2 kg/4½ lb

Minted blackberry and apple chutney

Metric	Imperial
1 kg blackberries	2 lb blackberries
1 kg cooking apples, peeled, cored and chopped	2 lb cooking apples, peeled, cored and chopped
1 kg onions, peeled and chopped	2 lb onions, peeled and chopped
grated rind and juice of 3 lemons	grated rind and juice of 3 lemons
1 × 15 ml spoon mixed spice	1 tablespoon mixed spice
2 × 5 ml spoons salt	2 teaspoons salt
4 × 15 ml spoons chopped mint	4 tablespoons chopped mint
600 ml red wine vinegar	1 pint red wine vinegar
500 g sugar	1 lb sugar

Cooking time: about 2 hours

Place all the ingredients in a large pan. Stir over a low heat until the sugar is dissolved. Bring to the boil, reduce the heat, then simmer for about 1½ hours, stirring occasionally, until the fruit is reduced to a pulp and the chutney is thick.
Sieve to remove the seeds if desired, then spoon while still hot into prepared jars. Seal with airtight, vinegar-proof covers.
Makes about 1¾ kg/4 lb

Banana and date chutney

Metric
1 kg bananas (6 large)
  sliced
1 kg cooking apples,
  peeled, cored and
  chopped
500 g dates, stoned and
  chopped
grated rind and juice
  of 2 large oranges
2 × 5 ml spoons mixed spice
2 × 5 ml spoons ground
  ginger
2 × 5 ml spoons curry
  powder
2 × 5 ml spoons salt
900 ml vinegar
500 g sugar

Imperial
2 lb bananas (6 large)
  sliced
2 lb cooking apples,
  peeled, cored and
  chopped
1 lb dates, stoned and
  chopped
grated rind and juice
  of 2 large oranges
2 teaspoons mixed spice
2 teaspoons ground
  ginger
2 teaspoons curry
  powder
2 teaspoons salt
1½ pints vinegar
1 lb sugar

Cooking time: about 1¼ hours

Place all the ingredients in a large pan. Stir over a low heat until the sugar is dissolved. Bring to the boil, reduce the heat, then simmer for about 1 hour, stirring occasionally, until the fruit is reduced to a pulp and the chutney is thick.
Spoon while still hot into prepared jars. Seal with airtight, vinegar-proof covers.
Makes about 2¾ kg/6 lb

Mint chutney

Metric
1 kg cooking apples,
  peeled, cored and
  chopped
1 kg onions, peeled
  and chopped
500 g tomatoes, peeled
  and quartered
225 g sultanas
grated rind and juice
  of 2 lemons
8 × 15 ml spoons chopped
  mint
4 × 15 ml spoons chopped
  parsley
600 ml cider vinegar
500 g granulated sugar
2 × 5 ml spoons salt

Imperial
2 lb cooking apples,
  peeled, cored and
  chopped
2 lb onions, peeled
  and chopped
1 lb tomatoes, peeled
  and quartered
8 oz sultanas
grated rind and juice
  of 2 lemons
8 tablespoons chopped
  mint
4 tablespoons chopped
  parsley
1 pint cider vinegar
1 lb granulated sugar
2 teaspoons salt

Cooking time: about 3 hours

This is a mild, fruity chutney and can be eaten almost immediately after making.

Place all the ingredients in a large pan. Stir over a low heat until the sugar is dissolved. Bring to the boil, reduce the heat and cook gently, stirring occasionally, until the fruit is reduced to a pulp and the chutney is thick. This will take about 1½ hours.
Spoon while still hot into prepared jars. Seal with airtight, vinegar-proof covers.
Makes about 2 kg/4½ lb

SAUCES AND RELISHES

Sauces and relishes can be served with hot and cold meats and savoury pastries, barbecued food, grilled meats and hamburgers, and are either poured over the food or spooned on to the side of the plate.

SAUCES

These use similar ingredients to chutneys, the difference being that the fruit and vegetables are usually sieved after cooking to give a smooth purée. They may vary from a smooth pouring sauce to a thicker condiment sauce to be served with meats or added to cooked dishes for flavouring.

Acidic sauces will keep without sterilizing but most sauces should be sterilized as for fruit bottling to keep them safely.

RELISHES

These are made just like chutneys but the cooking time is shorter so that the vegetables retain their shape. Because relishes are preserved with vinegar and sugar they do not need sterilizing. Fill and cover the jars as for pickles (see page 68).

FILLING SAUCE BOTTLES OR JARS

Pour the hot sauce into clean, dry, warm jars. Seal at once with screw-tops, boiled corks or Porosan preserving skin.

STERILIZING

Place the bottles in a deep pan on a trivet or other false bottom (see bottling on page 55); screw-tops should be slightly loose and corks secured with string or wire to allow steam and air to escape safely. Cover the bottles with hot, not boiling, water and bring slowly to simmering point, 88°C/190°F; hold it at this temperature for 30 minutes. Remove the bottles and secure the tops at once. Label and store the bottles in a cool, dry, dark place.

EQUIPMENT NEEDED

The same equipment is needed as for pickles and chutneys plus a sieve – preferably not metal as this may flavour the food – a liquidizer, bottles or jars.

Tomato and herb sauce

Metric	Imperial
1¾ kg tomatoes, quartered	4 lb tomatoes, quartered
350 g onions, peeled and chopped	12 oz onions, peeled and chopped
1 large sprig of rosemary	1 large sprig of rosemary
2 bay leaves	2 bay leaves
4 sprigs of mint	4 sprigs of mint
4 sprigs of thyme	4 sprigs of thyme
2 sprigs of sage	2 sprigs of sage
grated rind and juice of 2 lemons	grated rind and juice of 2 lemons
1 × 5 ml spoon salt	1 teaspoon salt
10 peppercorns	10 peppercorns
2 × 15 ml spoons soft brown sugar	2 tablespoons soft brown sugar

Cooking time: about 50 minutes

Serve with fish, lamb and pork.

Place all the ingredients in a saucepan, cover and bring to the boil slowly. Simmer, covered, for 30 minutes, stirring occasionally. Liquidize the sauce and sieve to a purée. Return to a clean pan and boil, uncovered, to reduce the sauce and thicken it until it coats the back of a wooden spoon. Reduce to 1.2 litres/2 pints. Taste and adjust the seasoning. Pour the sauce into prepared bottles or jars. Cover and sterilize. Label and store.
Makes 1.2 litres/2 pints

Barbecue sauce

Metric	Imperial
2 × 15 ml spoons oil	2 tablespoons oil
2 streaky bacon rashers, de-rinded and chopped	2 streaky bacon rashers, de-rinded and chopped
2 large onions, peeled and chopped	2 large onions, peeled and chopped
2 garlic cloves, peeled and crushed	2 garlic cloves, peeled and crushed
1 large carrot, peeled and sliced	1 large carrot, peeled and sliced
1 celery stick, chopped	1 celery stick, chopped
500 g cooking apples, peeled, cored and chopped	1 lb cooking apples, peeled, cored and chopped
1 kg tomatoes, quartered	2 lb tomatoes, quartered
1 thick slice lemon	1 thick slice lemon
2 bay leaves	2 bay leaves
1 cinnamon stick	1 cinnamon stick
1 thick slice root ginger	1 thick slice root ginger
10 peppercorns	10 peppercorns
8 cloves	8 cloves
1 mace blade	1 mace blade
2 chillies	2 chillies
2 × 15 ml spoons English mustard	2 tablespoons English mustard
300 ml malt vinegar	½ pint malt vinegar
100 g soft brown sugar	4 oz soft brown sugar
1 × 5 ml spoon salt	1 teaspoon salt

Cooking time: about 1 hour

Heat the oil in a large saucepan, then add the bacon, onion, garlic, carrot and celery. Fry for 5 minutes. Add the remaining ingredients, cover the pan and bring to the boil. Simmer, covered, for 45 minutes or until all the vegetables are soft, stirring occasionally to prevent sticking. Rub through a sieve to give a thick purée. Return the purée to a clean saucepan, taste and adjust the seasoning and bring to the boil. Pour the sauce into prepared jars or bottles, leaving 2½ cm/ 1 inch headspace. Cover and sterilize. Label and store.
Makes 1¾ litres/3 pints

Left: Tomato and herb sauce. Above: Barbecue sauce

Orange and Madeira sauce

Metric	Imperial
12 large oranges	12 large oranges
500 g granulated sugar	1 lb granulated sugar
300 ml wine vinegar	½ pint wine vinegar
600 ml Madeira	1 pint Madeira
600 ml water	1 pint water
3 × 15 ml spoons cornflour	3 tablespoons cornflour

Cooking time: about 35 minutes

Serve with duck, veal, ham and pork.

Grate the rind from 8 of the oranges and squeeze the juice. Cut away the peel and pith from the remaining 4 oranges and cut the flesh into segments. Place the sugar and vinegar in a saucepan and heat gently until the sugar dissolves. Boil for 5 minutes or until a brown caramel syrup is formed. Add the orange juice and rind, Madeira and water and simmer for about 10 to 15 minutes or until the liquid is reduced by a third.
Blend the cornflour with water to a thin paste, then pour into the sauce. Stir well until the sauce thickens and boils. Add the orange segments and simmer for 3 minutes. Cool slightly to distribute the orange pieces evenly, before pouring into prepared jars or bottles. Cover and sterilize. Label and store.
Makes 1½ litres/2½ pints

Spiced cranberry and walnut sauce

Metric	Imperial
4 large oranges	4 large oranges
225 g soft brown sugar	8 oz soft brown sugar
2 cinnamon sticks	2 cinnamon sticks
4 cloves	4 cloves
large pinch grated nutmeg	large pinch grated nutmeg
500 g cranberries	1 lb cranberries
100 g walnuts, chopped	4 oz walnuts, chopped

Cooking time: about 20 minutes

This makes a thick sauce on cooling. It can be spooned on to the side of a plate, and is particularly good with turkey.

Grate the rind of 2 oranges into a saucepan. Add the squeezed juice of all the oranges, then the sugar, cinnamon, cloves and nutmeg. Cook over low heat until the sugar dissolves, then bring to the boil.
Add the cranberries and simmer, uncovered, for 5 to 10 minutes or until the cranberries are just tender and the skins burst and the liquid has thickened slightly. Remove the cinnamon and cloves. Stir in the walnuts and pour into prepared jars or bottles. Tap the jars while filling to prevent air spaces. Cover and sterilize. Label and store.
Makes 1 kg/2 lb

Orange and Madeira sauce

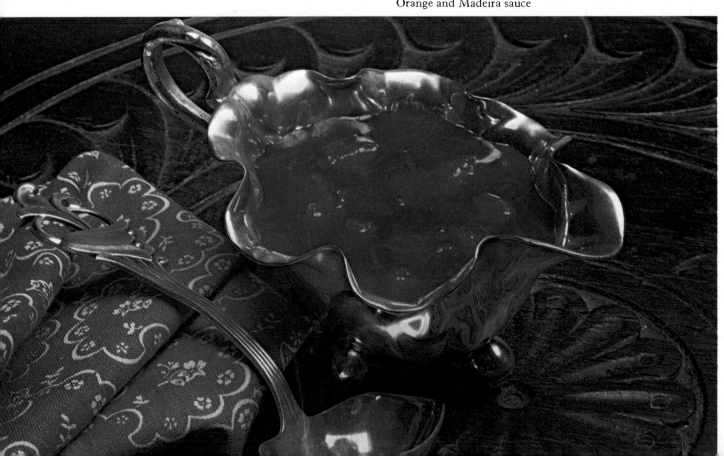

Cranberry and walnut sauce; Cumberland sauce

Cumberland sauce

Metric	Imperial
8 large oranges	8 large oranges
4 large lemons	4 large lemons
2 shallots, peeled	2 shallots, peeled
and finely chopped	and finely chopped
1 kg red currant jelly	2 lb red currant jelly
300 ml port	½ pint port
3 × 15 ml spoons cornflour	3 tablespoons cornflour

Cooking time: about 35 minutes

Serve cold with ham, pork and cold game pies.

Thinly cut the peel in large pieces from the oranges and lemons with a potato peeler. Cut into thin shreds and place in a small saucepan. Add the shallots and enough cold water to just cover. Bring to the boil, simmer for 5 minutes and drain.

Squeeze the juice from the oranges and lemons and place in a large saucepan with the red currant jelly and port. Heat gently to melt the jelly, then bring to the boil. Add the drained peel and shallots and simmer for 15 minutes until syrupy.

Blend the cornflour with water to a thin paste and pour into the sauce. Stir well until the sauce thickens and boils. Simmer for 2 minutes. Cool slightly to distribute the peel evenly, before pouring into prepared jars or bottles. Cover and sterilize. Label and store.

Makes 1½ litres/2½ pints

Mushroom duxelles sauce

Metric	Imperial
75 g butter	3 oz butter
225 g onions, peeled and finely chopped or grated	8 oz onions, peeled and finely chopped or grated
750 g flat mushrooms, finely chopped	1½ lb flat mushrooms, finely chopped
1 × 5 ml spoon dried mixed herbs	1 teaspoon dried mixed herbs
1 × 5 ml spoon paprika	1 teaspoon paprika
600 ml dry white wine	1 pint dry white wine
600 ml stock	1 pint stock
1 × 2.5 ml spoon salt	½ teaspoon salt
1 × 2.5 ml spoon ground pepper	½ teaspoon ground pepper
grated rind and juice of ½ large lemon	grated rind and juice of ½ large lemon

Cooking time: about 25 minutes

This makes a thick, concentrated mushroom sauce. It is often made in French cooking when it is used to flavour other sauces. It can also be used as a condiment sauce on the side of the plate.

Melt the butter in a saucepan, add the onion and fry gently for 5 minutes. Add the mushrooms and fry for 3 minutes, then add the herbs and paprika and fry for a further 3 minutes.
Add the wine, stock, salt and pepper and lemon rind and juice. Boil rapidly until nearly all the liquid has evaporated, but the mushrooms are still moist, to give a thick sauce. This will take about 15 minutes, depending on the size of the pan. Stir occasionally to prevent sticking, and frequently near the end, when most of the liquid has evaporated.
Spoon the sauce into prepared bottles or jars, pressing down well to prevent air spaces forming in the jars. Cover and sterilize. Label and store.
Makes 750 ml/1¼ pints

Apple and mint sauce

Metric	Imperial
1¾ kg cooking apples, peeled, cored and sliced	4 lb cooking apples, peeled, cored and sliced
grated rind and juice of 4 lemons	grated rind and juice of 4 lemons
300 ml water	½ pint water
100 g caster sugar	4 oz caster sugar
8 × 15 ml spoons chopped mint	8 tablespoons chopped mint

Cooking time: about 15 minutes

Serve with pork and poultry.

Place all the ingredients in a saucepan. Cover the pan and cook over a low heat for 15 minutes or until the apples are soft and reduced to a pulp. Stir occasionally to prevent sticking.
Liquidize or sieve the apples for a smooth sauce. Alternatively, beat the apples with a wooden spoon to form a purée, to give a more textured sauce. Pour the sauce into prepared jars or bottles. Cover and sterilize. Label and store.
Makes 1.2 litres/2 pints

From left: Mushroom duxelles sauce; Apple and mint sauce; Mint sauce; Horseradish sauce

Mint sauce

Metric	Imperial
225 g bunch of mint	*8 oz bunch of mint*
300 ml malt vinegar	*½ pint malt vinegar*

To serve: | *To serve:*
sugar | *sugar*
boiling water | *boiling water*
vinegar | *vinegar*
salt | *salt*
freshly ground pepper | *freshly ground pepper*

Sugar should not be added to mint for storing, as this could cause fermentation.

Wash and dry the mint, remove the leaves and discard the stalks. Chop the leaves and pack into clean, dry jars. Pour in sufficient vinegar to cover the mint. Seal the jars with vinegar proof covers. Label, then store in a cool dark place to preserve the colour of the mint.

Alternatively, place the mint leaves in a liquidizer goblet with the vinegar. Blend at a low speed until the mint is chopped. If a layer of foam forms at the top, skim this off. Pour the chopped mint and vinegar into jars as above.

To serve, remove as much mint as required and re-seal the jar. Add a little sugar, boiling water, vinegar, and salt and pepper to taste.

Horseradish sauce

Metric	Imperial
1–2 large horseradish	*1–2 large horseradish*
* roots*	* roots*
distilled vinegar	*distilled vinegar*

To serve: | *To serve:*
150 ml double cream, | *¼ pint double cream,*
*   soured cream or yogurt* | *   soured cream or yogurt*
salt | *salt*
freshly ground pepper | *freshly ground pepper*

Wash and peel the horseradish roots. Grate or shred the horseradish, keeping it well away from the eyes (it is even more pungent than onions). Pack immediately into clean, dry jars, then cover with vinegar to preserve the white colour. Seal the jars with vinegar-proof covers and store in a cool dark place.

To serve, remove 3 × 15 ml spoons/3 tablespoons of the concentrated grated horseradish, draining off the vinegar, then re-seal the jar. Stir in the cream, soured cream or yogurt and season to taste with salt and pepper.

Red relish

Metric	Imperial
1 kg tomatoes, skinned and quartered	2 lb tomatoes, skinned and quartered
1 kg red peppers, seeded and finely chopped	2 lb red peppers, seeded and finely chopped
500 g onions, peeled and chopped	1 lb onions, peeled and chopped
2 red chillies, very finely chopped	2 red chillies, very finely chopped
450 ml red wine vinegar	¾ pint red wine vinegar
200 g soft brown sugar	6 oz soft brown sugar
4 × 15 ml spoons mustard seed	4 tablespoons mustard seed
2 × 15 ml spoons celery seed	2 tablespoons celery seed
2 × 15 ml spoons paprika pepper	2 tablespoons paprika pepper
2 × 5 ml spoons salt	2 teaspoons salt
2 × 5 ml spoons coarsely ground black pepper	2 teaspoons coarsely ground black pepper

Cooking time: about 35 minutes

Place all the ingredients in a large saucepan and bring to the boil slowly. Simmer, uncovered, until most of the liquid has evaporated to give a thick, but moist consistency. This will take about 30 minutes, depending on the size of the pan. Stir more frequently as the liquid evaporates. Pour the relish into prepared jars or bottles. Seal with a vinegar-proof cover. Label and store.
Makes 1½ kg/3 lb

Sweetcorn relish

Metric	Imperial
600 ml white wine vinegar	1 pint white wine vinegar
75 g granulated sugar	3 oz granulated sugar
1 × 15 ml spoon mustard seed or 1 × 5 ml spoon dry mustard	1 tablespoon mustard seed or 1 teaspoon dry mustard
1 × 5 ml spoon salt	1 teaspoon salt
500 g sweetcorn kernels, fresh or frozen	1 lb sweetcorn kernels, fresh or frozen
1 green pepper, seeds removed and finely chopped	1 green pepper, seeds removed and finely chopped
1 red pepper, seeds removed and finely chopped	1 red pepper, seeds removed and finely chopped
1 onion, peeled and finely chopped	1 onion, peeled and finely chopped
100 g celery, finely sliced	4 oz celery, finely sliced

Cooking time: about 25 minutes

Mix a little of the vinegar with the sugar, mustard and salt to give a smooth paste, then stir in the rest of the vinegar. Pour the mixture into a saucepan and bring slowly to the boil. Add the vegetables to the pan. Simmer, uncovered, for 20 minutes or until the vegetables are just tender. Pour into prepared jars or bottles. Seal with a vinegar-proof cover. Label and store.
Makes about 1 kg/2 lb

From left: Gooseberry and almond relish; Tomato, apple and orange relish; Sweetcorn relish; Red relish

Tomato, apple and orange relish

Metric	Imperial
350 g soft brown sugar	12 oz soft brown sugar
300 ml cider or white wine vinegar	½ pint cider or white wine vinegar
grated rind and juice of 2 large oranges	grated rind and juice of 2 large oranges
25 g root ginger, peeled and finely chopped	1 oz root ginger, peeled and finely chopped
500 g tomatoes, chopped	1 lb tomatoes, chopped
500 g cooking apples, peeled, cored and finely chopped	1 lb cooking apples, peeled, cored and finely chopped
500 g onions, peeled and finely chopped	1 lb onions, peeled and finely chopped

Cooking time: about 40 minutes

Place the sugar, vinegar, orange rind and juice and ginger in a saucepan. Bring to the boil slowly. Add the tomatoes, apples and onions to the pan. Simmer, uncovered, for about 30 minutes or until most of the liquid has evaporated. Pack into prepared jars or bottles. Seal with vinegar-proof covers. Label and store.
Makes about 1½ kg/3½ lb

Gooseberry and almond relish

Metric	Imperial
50 g butter	2 oz butter
225 g onions, peeled and chopped	8 oz onions, peeled and chopped
100 g blanched split almonds	4 oz blanched split almonds
1 kg gooseberries, topped and tailed	2 lb gooseberries, topped and tailed
225 g granulated sugar	8 oz granulated sugar
300 ml white wine vinegar	½ pint white wine vinegar
1 × 2.5 ml spoon ground nutmeg	½ teaspoon ground nutmeg

Cooking time: about 35 minutes

Melt the butter in a saucepan. Add the onion and almonds and fry gently until the almonds are lightly browned, stirring lightly. Add the remaining ingredients and bring slowly to the boil. Simmer, uncovered, for 30 minutes or until most of the liquid has evaporated. Spoon into prepared jars or bottles. Seal with vinegar-proof covers. Label and store.
Makes 1.2 litres/2 pints

Index